Policeman's Story

Harry Cole was born and brought up in Bermondsey, south London. He left school when he was fourteen, during the war, and became a cricket-bat maker, soldier, stonemason and, in 1952, a policeman. For thirty years, until he retired in 1983, he served at the same police station in London.

He is a qualified FA coach (he has run numerous junior football teams), a referee and a keen cricketer. For many years he had a regular column in the *Warren*, the police magazine. His other books are *Policeman's Progress* (1980), *Policeman's Lot* (1981), *Policeman's Patch* (1982) and *Policeman's Patrol* (1983), and the first volume of his autobiography, *Policeman's Prelude* (1984).

Harry Cole is married and has a daughter. In 1978 he was awarded the British Empire Medal for voluntary work. Since leaving the force, in addition to writing he has taken up after-dinner speaking.

D1041193

Harry Cole

Policeman's Story

Fontana Paperbacks

First published in 1985 by Fontana Paperbacks,
8 Grafton Street, London W1X 3LA

Printed and bound in Great Britain by
William Collins Sons & Co. Ltd, Glasgow

For Christine

Contents

1. Twenty-one pay pontoons only

'You're late!'

I looked up at the ancient brown-framed clock, ticking loudly across the green-tiled entrance hall. I suppose three minutes after nine was a little late – three minutes, to be precise.

'Well, it is only three minutes,' I protested.

'*Only* three minutes! *Only*? Do you know what it is possible to accomplish in three minutes? Well, do you?'

'Well, er, of course I do.' I paused, searching desperately for an answer. Given half an hour with pen and paper, I bet I could have produced a positive ream of three-minute accomplishments. The only one that entered my head at that precise moment, however, was the lavatory. 'I'm sorry but I had to go to the toilet.'

'That's it, then, is it? That's the answer you think will suffice? You had to go to the toilet?'

'Well, there was the bus as well. It was a bit late because of the fog.'

He studied me at some length. 'You know, it strikes me that if by some mischance you complete this training course, the customary smooth running of the Metropolitan Police will seem doubly threatened, firstly by the irregularities of the 36 bus to Victoria and secondly, and even more alarmingly, by your unpredictable bowel movements. You live the nearest and yet you are the last to arrive, did you know that?'

I resisted the urge to point out that if I was the last to arrive, then how could I possibly know it. 'Er – no, I didn't.'

'You have – let me see.' He dropped his head momentarily to study his clipboard. 'You have a journey of exactly one and a quarter miles – and yet you arrive late! We have two men on this course who originate from the Hebrides, yet they arrive punctually. Can you explain that?'

I thought his whole stance was illogical but I decided against beginning my new career in the force with an argument, especially with the first police sergeant I had ever actually spoken to. He rightly took my silence as a concession and returned to his clipboard.

'Right, I'll tell you what I am going to do with you. I am going to resist the temptation to show you the door – although that would probably be the best thing for the force – instead you will forfeit seniority. Your warrant number was to have been 138680 but now I am going to put that back ten digits. You will now be 138690. This warrant number will stay with you for the whole of your police service. It will never now change from this day.' He nodded to himself, obviously well satisfied with his decision.

I thought it seemed a hell of a fuss over three minutes and I was not even sure what he was talking about. Still, if it removed the determined Sergeant Cassidy from my back, then I considered it ten digits well spent.

'Right, pick up your suitcase and follow me, left-right-left-right . . .'

Appearances were everything to Sergeant Cassidy. He could spot an unfastened button around three corners. He was right about my punctuality, though, it had always been my problem. I wondered what a loss of seniority actually meant. Did it mean that I would one day be passed over for Commissioner, because I was ten places back in antiquity?

As Cassidy had rightly said, our basement flat was a little over a mile away from the training school, yet in reality I felt as far from home as either of our two Hebrideans. The feeling had nothing to do with distance but a great deal to do with background. With my origins and instincts, I could not have been more unsure if I had joined the Foreign Legion. Perhaps I should have told Cassidy to stuff his job and legged it down to Victoria? I could, after all, be home inside twenty minutes. I was still indecisive when, some fifteen minutes later, we were led into a classroom. There twenty-two of us took an oath of allegiance and I felt instantly more settled.

The Metropolitan Police Training School at Peel House near Victoria was, on a good day, slightly inferior to a dockland dosshouse. Certainly many buildings and institutions in postwar London were a compromise, but Peel House always gave me the impression it was chosen as a police training school by a conglomeration of mastercrooks. It was cramped, badly lit and had all the comforts of a medieval plague-pit.

For three months recruits would be saturated with law, first-aid, law, self-defence, law and then more law. The first item of equipment issued would be the Metropolitan Police Instruction Book, or IB, as it was more usually called. This book was similar in size to Kelly's Street Directory and just about as readable. It contained every piece of information that a young constable – or an old one for that matter – would need to know. There were hundreds of pages in the thing and sizeable chunks of them had to be learnt word-perfect.

To the rare visitor, Peel House must have looked like an asylum. Strange, chanting people would wander in and out of rooms and corridors, frequently with their eyes shut tight in concentration. Holding their black books in front of them, they would recite to themselves throughout the whole evening and even half the night. The heavy doors and great thick walls simply added to this feeling of forced institutionalism. Even our expeditions to the outside world did little to help. It is true we were allowed out at any time but pressure of studies kept these excursions down to a weekly swim and a fortnightly hair-cut.

It was the pure process of learning so much parrot-fashion that I found the most difficult of all. To retain masses of boring acts and sections in my brain, when I really ached to know the latest football scores, was pure agony. My inability to retain, or even understand most of it, caused my self-confidence to plummet.

Each week a revision test was held and marks awarded. To fail this test meant a back-squadding, i.e., being placed in the class behind. To fail two tests meant OUT. A league-table based on the results of these tests was soon drawn up. In three months out of twenty-two positions I never once rose above nineteenth place!

Perhaps my worst moment was one Sunday midway through the course. I had gone home for the weekend, and my wife Joan and I sat around the fireside while she tested me on various pieces that I was expected to know. I faltered through the chapter and verse of the thing while she helped me with the occasional key word. The subject of her questioning related to the action to be taken by any constable unfortunate enough to discover a dead body in the street. True, the discovery of such a corpse sitting quietly on the pavement was not expected to be a daily occurrence. On the other hand, it was far more likely than the next subject – sheep-dipping!

I stuttered and started some half-dozen times, before I furiously gave up with the words, 'Sod it! How does it go?'

'"When bodies of persons found dead in the street . . ."' she began, and then carried on the tedious transcript for some two hundred more words. Depressed with my inabilities, I looked up at her dejectedly. Instantly I felt like killing her! She was no longer reading it! She knew it! She actually knew the bloody thing! She had learnt it parrot-fashion while testing me!

Snatching the book from her lap, I threw it into the burning grate. Metropolitan Police Instruction Books, however, were sturdy items and virtually indestructible. They needed to be, bearing in mind the mental condition of their average reader. Joan hastily retrieved the book without it sustaining as much as a scorch. Dusting it quickly, she resumed her seat and smiled at me as if nothing had happened.

'Now once more: "When bodies of persons . . ."' she prompted.

I sighed, but responded, '"Found dead in the street . . ." er, what comes next?'

'Tea, I think,' she said.

Of course, not all recruits had this sort of problem. It was usually those of us who had been manual workers who experienced the most difficulty. Janie Johnson, for example, was one of three girls in the class. She not only found time to look extremely attractive and immaculately groomed, but she was consistently top of the league-table *and* learnt her part in the school Christmas musical, *Call me Madam*. Oh, how I hated Janie.

As if the course was not already difficult enough, about halfway through first-aid was introduced. Some fifteen or so lessons were sprinkled throughout the middle weeks of the course. The instructor for this diversion was doubly unique: Sergeant William Barrington-Fairweather looked like Hermann Goering and acted like Adolf Hitler. To fail to answer a question in Sergeant Barrington-Fairweather's class seemed to be taken as a personal affront to his dignity – not just to his but his whole rotten family's. If I could not separate a concussion from a compression – and I never could – then I always had the feeling that I was condemning every one of the Barrington-Fairweathers to a life of abject pain and misery.

'What would you do for a concussion, Cole?'

'Er, undo his clothing, sarge?'

'I'm not sure if you're a nudist or a flaming pooftah but it strikes me that whenever you don't know the answer to a first-aid question, then all you think you have to do is to take off the poor sod's clothing!'

His eyes would bulge as he placed his full, fat face inches

from mine. His voice, normally quite resonant, would rise an octave after every sentence and he would glower – such a glower!

'If you don't sort this out by tomorrow you are out, d'you understand? O-U-T, out!'

Usually at this stage he would pivot around to seek the first smirk. Woe betide anyone he caught wearing one! He would rush over to them and scream out some obscure first-aid question about opium-poisoning, or such like. For me, this was the best part of the first-aid lecture. One thing about Barrington-Fairweather, he never came to anyone twice during a fifty-minute period. There were twenty-two students in that class and fifty minutes was not really very long to be objectionable to them all.

Our twenty-two recruits reduced to twenty by the sixth week. Both Hebrideans returned to Skye or some such place. It was not a mutual decision on their part – in fact they did not get on too well together – they simply upped and left within days of each other.

Perhaps one reason for their departure was that we had by then the reputation of being a difficult class. This was not altogether our fault. Our first instructor, the cheerful red-faced Sergeant Hatton, fell sick after only one week. The same fate befell our second. The third was hastily transferred from the school over some matter concerning the left thigh of a lady recruit. The result was that, barely halfway through our course, we were already on our fourth instructor.

This constant changing made life very difficult for everyone. The rapport needed between the instructor and his class can only develop with time. What happened in our class was that any sergeant returning from sick or annual leave promptly copped our class. Our overall progress, with the honourable exception of the fair Miss Johnson, was not good. In fact it bordered on the disastrous. In short, we were bad news for any instructor. Perhaps the brightest spots in the whole three months were the practical demonstrations. We always enjoyed these because it meant being away from the accursed instruction book. The instructors, too, clearly enjoyed them. It gave them a chance to show off any acting ability they believed they possessed. They played judges and ponces; vicars and tarts; hairy-chested lesbians and highly dubious sailors. They played nuns and whores; members of Parliament and meths-drinking tramps and, on occasions, they even played policemen. One thing was sure, if the instructors ever ganged up on a recruit, then he or she would never forget it. Whatever the flaw in a recruit's approach to a situation, it would be mercilessly explored by these frustrated thespians.

I had a particular weakness which was consistently shown up during the mock-court sittings that were held in our classroom. For some unaccountable reason, I would omit to look at the magistrate. Whenever I took a classroom oath, the instructor would be heard entreating me, 'Will you *look* at the bloody magistrate, Cole!'

The culmination of all these classroom practices eventually took place in the gym towards the end of the course. An incident would be set up, in which each recruit had arrested a miscreant – always belligerently played by another instructor – and brought him before the court. Several classes would be involved in this operation; many recruits as well as instructors would take part as bit-players. For the inexperienced policeman a court appearance can be nerve-racking. None however is quite so terrifying as the very first one in front of half of the personnel at the training school. As each recruit awaited their turn to enter the box and give evidence, they would visibly shake.

In my case, I had been required to arrest a scruffy-looking individual (Sergeant George Hoskins from class 6Z) for being a 'pedlar without a licence'. Now illegal peddling was not actually rife in London at the time. In fact, I never saw another during the next thirty years I was to spend in the force (perhaps they all went sheep-dipping).

However, Frederick Arthur Ronald Taylor (pedlars always gave great thought to their initials) pleaded not guilty and stated he would be calling several witnesses. The court then prepared itself for a contested case.

While F. A. R. Taylor made his plea, I frantically ran over in my mind as many facts about the arrest as I could. Finally there was a hush in the court and everyone turned expectantly towards me. I was dry-mouthed and petrified.

'Hold the book in your right hand and repeat after me,' droned the usher, 'I swear by almighty God . . .' He paused.

'I-I swear by almighty G-God . . .'

'That the evidence I give this court . . .' I seriously questioned my chances of repeating another six words. My throat had all but seized up. I croaked and forced a painful cough.

'Is something wrong, officer?' asked the magistrate in a bored, condescending voice.

'N-no, sir,' I answered, firing off yet another pair of nervous coughs. 'I've just got a dodgy throat, that's all.'

'Well, d'you think you could persuade your "dodgy throat" to get on with it? I do have a long list this morning and we haven't got all day.'

I stupidly decided to give one great final cough, in the futile hope that this would improve my audibility. All that happened was that my tonsils cracked against the roof of my mouth and left me in such pain that I seriously wondered if I would ever speak again.

'That the evidence I give this court . . .' persisted the usher.

'That . . . the . . . evidence . . . I . . . give . . . this . . . court.' The strangulated words had the fluency and pitch of a rusty winch.

'Mr Sinclair!' exploded the magistrate. 'Is this the prosecution's only witness?'

'Yes, Your Worship,' nodded the 'prosecuting counsel'. 'Not very good, is he?'

16

'Not very good! He's utterly appalling! He's like a eunuch with the pox!'

A nervous titter ran around the twenty young recruits sitting behind me. I somehow struggled through the rest of the oath.

'Officer, as I am the magistrate of this court, will you kindly look at me whilst offering your evidence? You see, I have this strange desire to be noticed. And now, providing your dodgy throat has recovered, perhaps we can get on?' He turned his attention once more to the prosecuting counsel. 'Yes, Mr Sinclair?'

'Your Worship,' acknowledged Sinclair courteously, as he rose to his feet and glanced quickly down at his notes. 'Officer, were you on duty in the High Street, W1, at ten-thirty yesterday morning?'

'Y-yes, sir.'

'Would you tell the court exactly what you saw there?'

'Well, sir, I s-saw him, I mean the prisoner – Taylor.'

'Yes, yes,' replied the prosecution irritably. 'But what was he doing there?'

'H-he was ringing on doorbells, sir.'

The defence counsel rocketed to his feet. 'Ringing on doorbells, eh?' he mimicked. 'Is this perhaps some new parliamentary statute of which the court is unaware? Has some eccentric select committee forced through a new offence of "ringing-on-doorbells"? How about knocking-on-knockers and walking-up-steps, will they now be declared offences too?'

Although I thought that was particularly silly, I could only bleat, 'N-no, sir.'

My mind was by this time a total blank. I somehow had a recollection that as a pedlar the prisoner should have had a certificate, but for the life of me I could not shape my thoughts into coherent words.

'He w-was doing it without a c-certificate, sir,' I finally blurted out.

'Oh! He was doing it without a certificate, was he? Oh,

well, that puts an entirely different light upon it. Why did you not say so in the first place? What a dastardly chap my client is, to be sure! Ringing doorbells without a certificate, whatever will they do next? Tell me, officer –' his voice dropped confidentially and he winked knowingly at me – 'just how many doorbells did he ring?'

I was slowly losing the whole thing and I knew it. 'Er – it w-was several, sir.'

'Oh, it was several, was it?' He nodded understandingly and looked slowly around the whole court. 'And exactly *how* many is "several"? One? Two? Four and a half thousand?'

Even after all these years I could burst into tears at the sheer embarrassment of it. Suddenly there was a reprieve – well, it was a reprieve of sorts.

'Twenty-one, pay pontoons only!' The excited voice cut through my mental fog. I turned towards the bench and was amazed to see His Worship wearing a party hat and smoking a big cigar, in the process of laying down a pair of playing cards on the desk in front of him. I could clearly see the ace of clubs and jack of diamonds.

'Blast!' exclaimed the clerk of the court in a loud voice. 'I had a bloody good hand, too!'

I closed my eyes and wished myself a million miles away. Of course I had forgotten to look at the magistrate! In fact I had barely glanced at him since the case had begun.

'Case dismissed and costs awarded against the officer for failing to spot I had pontoon,' announced His Worship. 'Next case!'

As a result of that verdict, F. A. R. Taylor, alias George Hoskins, doorbell ringer *extraordinaire*, walked from that court a free man – and I never ceased staring at magistrates.

One week later, to my surprise and Barrington-Fairweather's total astonishment, I passed my first-aid exam, albeit with an enormous amount of luck. My 'patient' had been Taffy Reece, a former nurse and a right Johnny-know-all. He had whispered directions to me throughout the whole of his 'treatment' and, more important, he had been correct. A classic case of a physician healing himself.

No matter how well a student did at first-aid, however, there was still the reckoning of the overall final exam. There would be no helpful whispers there. To have any hope of passing, I would need to concentrate on just fifty per cent of the work we had been given to absorb. In this way I considered I had a 50/50 chance of becoming a policeman. Any other way I was out of work.

Two weeks before the final exam, it suddenly appeared I would not perhaps be staying after all. My wife Joan and I had what is nowadays known as a cash-flow problem. At the time we just thought we were skint. Recruits were paid each Wednesday lunchtime and on that evening I would hop on a 36 bus to take home the lion's share of my £5 10s wages. I would leave the school just after rush-hour and was always back in time for three hours' study before lights-out at eleven o'clock. Unfortunately the winter of 1952–3 was London's foggiest ever and, although I managed to struggle home, the fog blanketed in and it was impossible to return. I decided, therefore, to stay home for the night and try once more at daybreak. Now although recruits were allowed to wander freely outside the precincts of Peel House, doors were locked and lights went out sharp at eleven o'clock. Even Cinderella was allowed an hour longer. Shortly after midnight, therefore, when the duty sergeant made his rounds, there was just one empty bed – mine.

When I tiptoed into the building just before breakfast next morning, I had no idea of the fuss that I had caused. Our intrepid sergeant, on finding the empty bed, had promptly woken the surrounding sleepers and sent them over the building in search of the absconder. I was not popular. Nothing at first was said to me officially. The grapevine, however, never stopped sending out signals. They let me sweat it out all morning in the classroom, then just after midday, I was told to report to the chief superintendent. At first I could not believe the way he went on. For twenty minutes he barely stopped. He reiterated how the force wanted reliable, responsible men and how I had let it down. In fact, not only had I let down the force, but I had let down him, the instructors and even all my classmates. At one stage I expected him to announce that he had notified the Commissioner, Home Secretary and Winston Churchill.

'But I only took my wages home, sir!' I protested.

'Ah yes, this week your wages, but how about next week, eh? What will the excuse be then? After all, we don't actually *know* that you went home, do we? You could have gone *anywhere*, couldn't you?'

'Not on five and a half quid I couldn't.' I realized my mistake the instant I said those words. He was on to them in a flash. His mood changed immediately from reproach to aggression.

'I see! So the pay isn't good enough for you, eh? What do you think you are worth, then?' He looked down at the file in front of him. 'Judging by your overall course marks, I would say not a lot. But then perhaps you disagree?'

I was neatly in a trap. The only consolation was that at least I realized it. Now struck me as being a very good time to say nothing. There was a prolonged silence before he finally spoke.

'You have no more to say, then?'

'No, sir.' I said even that reluctantly.

'Very well, I'll give you the benefit of the doubt,' he said graciously, as if he were awarding me the Queen's Police Medal. 'But you understand, one more slip, however slight, and you are out. The Metropolitan Police is no place for unreliable characters. Right, cut along to your classroom and from now on I will expect a great improvement in your classwork. That's all.'

For the rest of the afternoon I boiled with frustration, and my customary evening-long studies were a complete waste of time. I was perilously close to resigning. I think I only didn't because I felt I should have resigned during my interview. Then I could at least have spoken my mind. However, after a weekend at home and some fireside revision, it was back to normal on the Monday, for the last lap of the course.

The only thing I can remember with any clarity about the exam classroom is the smell of the floor-polish; the place reeked of it.

'No talking or leaving the room,' growled the chief inspector. 'If you want anything, just raise your hand and wait, an instructor will attend you. You now have ten seconds to go. Turn your papers over . . . seven, eight, nine . . . now!'

As the rustle of paper swept through the room, little moans of disappointment together with gasps of delight could be heard. I, for one, could not believe my good fortune. Every question on the paper was from the half of the curriculum that I had studied! I just could not stop writing!

Later that day, when the first of the marks were announced, I discovered that out of a possible 120 I had scored 117. My delight was rather diluted in the chief superintendent's ten-minute chat afterwards. '. . . and as for you, Cole, there is no doubt in my mind that our little talk made the world of difference to your final efforts. I think I can rightly claim all due credit, don't you?'

It was obvious from his tone that he did not expect an answer to this fatuous observation. Which, all in all, was just as well, really. I would hate to have been the first recruit ever to resign simply because he passed the exam.

2. Stonemasons, freemasons

After the rigours of the three-month course, successful recruits were given a week's leave. The unsuccessful were back-squadded and had to resit the exam two weeks later. Four of our class had failed and one of them, Derek Marshall, took it quite badly. I felt that he blamed me for his misfortune. It is true that he had been consistently in the first three positions of the weekly league-table. However, these tables were simply a guide and counted for nothing on exam day. The fact that I had managed to pass the exam after three months of struggling at the bottom of the class seemed to infuriate Derek.

'Would you have felt better if I had failed?' I asked, in a burst of exasperation.

'Well, yes. Yes, I would,' he replied, with forced jocularity. 'It would certainly have made more sense.'

In different circumstances, I would have been unable to resist a thundering good gloat. Yet I felt sorry for him because he had put in an enormous amount of work. In addition, I realized just how fortunate I had been. Derek never really recovered from that original disappointment; within weeks of finally passing the exam, he became the first of our class to resign. I have always been surprised at the number of recruits who do this. Having sweated blood for three months, it seems a terrible waste to resign before the ink has dried on the warrant card.

After our week's leave, and on a bright crisp March morning, we all reported back to the training school. After a short pep talk from the chief superintendent we were each given our postings. While waiting for transport we took the opportunity to say our goodbyes. We pledged life-long friendships and faithfully promised one another that we would stay in touch.

A ramshackle old coach finally collected us and dropped us in groups at our new stations. Within hours, twelve of my newly sworn friends had dropped out of my life forever.

Jimmy Davenport, Peter Ward and I were posted to Carter Street in south London. I was not too happy about this, primarily because I lived on the manor and had visions of troubled neighbours knocking on my door at all hours. While I was certainly prepared to give the force a daily eight hours, there was no way that I saw the job as a calling. If society wanted a twenty-four-hour-day policeman, then it was going to have to offer me far more than the going rate of six quid a week.

Carter Street Police Station itself is something of a misnomer. Although it is named Carter Street, it is not situated in Carter *Street* but in Carter *Place*. In addition, its official address is 292 Walworth Road. As if finding the damned place is not difficult enough, it is also the only building in the area to sport a long garden, so it lies well back from the main road and is unseen by all except the determined seeker. The mystique concerning its location could also explain a great deal about its obscurity, for obscure it certainly is. Standing as it does about a mile and a half from Scotland Yard, it was, and is still, an extremely busy station in a high-crime area, with arrests running at thousands a year. Yet even within the Metropolitan Police Force itself, very few coppers seemed even to have heard of it. Station folklore (a notorious fund of misinformation) has it that way back in the distant past it was classified as a punishment station – allegedly places where discipline defaulters were sent to ponder on the error of their ways. Although I cannot vouch for the accuracy of these allegations, it is a fact that the first reaction of a newcomer to the station is usually: 'Good God, is this really a police station? How soon can I get a transfer?'

The building itself well typified the area at that time. It was cramped and decrepit, with toilet facilities slightly inferior to a Peruvian camel-yard. The rats that abounded in the stables and the mice that played freely in the clothing rooms made the nightly swarm of canteen cockroaches seem quite friendly. The chief inspector who ran the station sensibly lived in a flat on the top floor, presumably as far away as possible from the vermin playing so cheerfully in the basement. In spite of these little hygiene difficulties, thirty single officers sometimes slept in dormitories on the middle floors. I say 'sometimes slept' because sleeping above any busy police station is a dubious pleasure at the best of times, but this particular one also had a railway line running underneath its dormitory windows – to say nothing of the two humming great heaps of horse-manure steaming in the corner of the yard. Punishment station perhaps it was – and I was starting a thirty-year stretch!

Soon after arriving at the station, or 'nick' as it is usually known, we were ushered in to see 'The Guv'nor'. The Guv'nor was a big man in every respect, six feet four inches in height and the build of a heavyweight wrestler. He had a booming Scots voice and an awe-inspiring presence. He was never referred to by name but only by his tycoon-like initials. John O'Donnell, or rather 'Jay-Oh-Dee', was the most powerful man at the station. He could put fear into recruits by simply narrowing his eyes. Quite truthfully, he scared me stiff.

The old sergeant who had taken us as far as Jay-Oh-Dee's door had warned us to approach the great man 'with all due fear and trembling'. To this end our trio needed little coaxing: awe-struck, we stood before him. The great head was bent over a pile of correspondence and did not seem to be aware of our presence. I coughed nervously. Immediately – just for a split second – a piercing eye was raised in irritation. Strangely enough, the head itself did not seem to move – just the eye. I froze in response. After some minutes, the head slowly and majestically rose.

'Who are ye?'

Jay-Oh-Dee was as sparing with words as he was with money. We each waited for each other to be the first to speak. As a result there was total silence.

'Are ye deaf?' he boomed. 'Who are ye?'

Then of course we all babbled at once.

Leaning back in his chair he put down his pen. These twin movements had the combined majesty of Tower Bridge being raised.

We explained that we were three brand-new recruits eager to do battle with the capital's master criminals. He said nothing at first, but searched each of us thoroughly with his eyes. He started this visual examination with Jimmy Davenport, before progressing to me, then Peter Ward. Finally his eyes once more returned to Jimmy. He stared at him for at least a full minute and then shook his head so slightly that it was barely a perceptible movement. Nothing had been officially proved or said at the training school, but we had all suspected that Jim was homosexual. It had taken us weeks to arrive at that conclusion. Jay-Oh-Dee, I felt, had sussed it out in seconds.

'Reet, smarten yourselves, I'm taking ye to see the chief inspector.'

Big John O'Donnell was in fact nothing more than the chief inspector's clerk – but what a clerk! To all intents and purposes he ran the station, hence his nickname 'The Guv'nor'. He was responsible for allocating men to shifts (or 'reliefs', as they are known within the force), he was also responsible for pay, but his most powerful weapon was his responsibility for allocating paperwork enquiries to sergeants and inspectors. If any member of these two ranks had the courage, temerity or, perhaps, downright stupidity to upset PC John O'Donnell, then that man's locker would bulge with correspondence before the hour was out. This enquiry work would have to be undertaken in addition to the recipient's routine police work. Many sergeants would find they could only cope by taking their work home. O'Donnell could easily treble the workload of any man at the station whenever he chose. Nowadays all police stations have 'enquiry sections' of some twenty to thirty civilians who are busily engaged in the same tasks that Jay-Oh-Dee gleefully doled out to just a handful of men.

The three of us lined up in front of Chief Inspector James Hall. Again our interviewer was a big man, but tall rather than broad, this time with a huge moustache. He gave us the usual welcome-aboard speech but then surprised us greatly by adding, 'If there is ever anything you feel I should know, any conversation you may overhear in the canteen, for example, come directly up and see me. You'll not be the loser, I can assure you. Do you understand what I am saying to you?'

For the second time that day we each left it to the others to reply to a question. For the second time that day there was silence.

'Do *you* understand, Davenport?' persisted the chief inspector.

'Yessir,' nodded Jimmy quickly.

'Do *you* understand, Ward?'

Peter was nodding almost before the question was finished, 'Yessir.'

'And do *you* understand, Cole?'

'Yessir.'

I understood right enough: this man was inviting the three of us to be a fifth column. He obviously expected us to spy on our new colleagues at our very first station! But why?

'Mr O'Donnell will tell you which relief you are to be posted to. That is all.'

We filed out, and again had to wait some minutes for Jay-Oh-Dee to raise his great head from the desk. Eventually I was told I was to be posted night-duty, during which time I was to 'learn beats'. Jimmy was to be posted on the same

26

relief as myself, while Peter was to be early-turn. Just as we were about to leave the office, Jay-Oh-Dee told us to button up our greatcoats the correct way. I glanced down at the three coats and they each appeared correct in every detail.

'But we have,' I pointed out.

'Ye have *not*, laddie!' thundered the huge Scot angrily. 'I dinna talk for talking's sake, y'know!' With that he thrust the office copy of General Orders across the table at me. There it was quite clearly stated that beginning on the first day of each month, all greatcoats must be fastened up on the alternate side. This was, incredibly enough, to prevent wear and tear on the buttonholes!

'Wear and tear on the buttonholes!' exclaimed Peter Ward. 'You couldn't wear-an'-tear these buttonholes with a blowtorch. Just look at them, they're bombproof!'

'I dinna make the rules, laddie, I'm simply advising ye.'

That was good enough for me. 'Advice' from Jay-Oh-Dee was like divine inspiration from anyone else.

Rebuttoning our coats, we descended the staircase. Once out of earshot of the office, we excitedly asked each other of the significance of the chief inspector's speech. Of course, we knew the implications of it, but we had no idea what could be behind it. What sort of station was this, we wondered, in which almost the first words spoken to us was an invitation to spy on our new colleagues?

To learn beats on night-duty is a mixed blessing: the quieter tempo of the early hours does assist one to adjust; on the other hand, much of the manor is closed or asleep. However, it wasn't the manor which interested me. I knew it quite well anyway. What I needed was an introduction to the men who patrolled it – and that was not easily forthcoming. The aloofness and even occasional downright rudeness of many old coppers in their attitude to recruits took me completely by surprise.

At that time – 1953 – there was still a fair number of older, prewar policemen patrolling the streets. Most of these men were totally different from those who joined after the war. They were particularly secretive about all aspects of their work. 'You're lucky if they tell you the time,' complained Peter Ward ruefully. To some of them, to wander either accidentally or intentionally on to another man's beat was tantamount to running away with his wife. There were in fact a few men who would have sooner lost their wife than their beat. They were always suspicious and it took a long time to break down this distrust. A recruit would need to be at a station for well over a year, preferably two, before he was finally accepted into the fold. In some cases he would never be accepted at all. There were several reasons for this, the main one probably being the length of time the average copper served at a station – usually a decade or more. Rather as in a small village, everyone was regarded as a newcomer for the first eight years. Today a recruit is accepted as soon as he or she arrives, and anyone with more than two years' street-duty behind them is considered a veteran. This is because there are now so many other specialized fields open to them. Before the sixties, however, matters were very different. If, for example, a man failed, or never sat, the promotion exam, he had few options. There were no bomb squads, drug squads, porn squads, crime squads, embassy protection squads, burglary squads, robbery squads, special patrol groups, instant response units, collators, juvenile bureaus or community coppers. In fact the choice was simple: one could take promotion or become the station cyclist. Of course, the latter perk was not to be sneered at, paying as it did sixpence for wear and tear on one's bike.

In effect, the old-time copper prided himself on being able to deal with anything that came up, without having to refer it to a 'squad'. Of course, he would be far happier if he could hoist it on to the bloke on the next beat. Failing that, if he walked into it – whatever 'it' was – then he would consider he could cope.

Because of my local knowledge, my period of learning beats was cut to just one week and I was soon to be out on my own. Even as a brand-new recruit, I had already begun to feel that the atmosphere at the station was not quite right. I could not put my finger on it but I somehow never felt at ease there. On my last night of learning beats, I took my courage in my hands and asked my companion, George Rearsden, a man with some twenty years' experience, what, if anything, was wrong. He said nothing for a few moments but walked silently alongside me.

'How old're you?' he suddenly asked.

'Twenty-two.'

'You always lived local?'

I nodded.

'Why'd you join?'

'It was that or be out of work, I s'pose.'

Again there was a prolonged silence.

Suddenly he took me by the arm and almost thrust me into a deep dark doorway.

'Tell me, why did you tell everyone you were a mason, eh?'

I was taken aback for a moment and quite surprised at his sudden aggression. 'I didn't know that I *had* told everyone.'

'You mentioned it in the canteen. That's like telling everyone. Why did you admit it so openly, eh?'

'Well, I *was* most certainly a mason, but I didn't know it was something one "admitted" to.'

George seemed genuinely puzzled by my attitude. 'It's just that I have never before heard anyone actually admit to being one. I've always found masons to be so bloody secretive.'

'Wait a minute!' I responded, the penny finally dropping. 'Are you talking about freemasons?'

'Of course. What else d'you think I'm on about?'

'I was a *stonemason*! That was my job. I whacked bloody great lumps of stone with a mallet and a chisel!'

'Oh, I see!' He laughed a rare laugh. 'That explains a lot. The blokes on the relief couldn't understand it. Normally we never know who these buggers are, then you come along and promptly announce that you are one! That's why the blokes were so suspicious. In any case, that's not all of it.'

'What else is there then?'

George did not answer at first but thrust both his hands in his overcoat pockets and rummaged around for a few seconds. He then withdrew a smooth square tin containing tobacco and papers. In a practised, solemn ritual, he rolled himself a thin cigarette.

'Did Jimmy have a word with you? When you first come here, I mean.'

'Yes, he did.'

'Did he ask you to report to him anything that you might have heard? Canteen conversation and such like. Or anything for instance that the men might have said?'

'Yes, he did.'

'What d'you think about that, then?'

'Not a lot. In fact I think it's appalling.'

His cigarette, now little more than a wisp, had gone out. Although barely an inch of it was left, he tilted his head to one side and relit it. He sniffed, gave a couple of tight-lipped puffs and turned his attention once more to me.

'Jimmy-the-one, he's a Trenchard-Boy. That's what's really the matter with this nick,' he announced. 'If we could only get rid of him, you wouldn't know the place in a couple of weeks.'

'What on earth is a Trenchard-Boy?' I asked in genuine puzzlement.

'You've joined the force and you don't know what a bloody Trenchard-Boy is? You mean to say you know sod-all about the greatest bleedin' disaster ever to hit this job? Don't you know nothin'?'

I shrugged, frightened to use any words that might antagonize my new companion. Already he had spoken more in a few minutes than the rest of those prewar coppers in all the time since I joined.

'Trenchard was Commissioner in the mid-thirties,' he explained. 'The only problem with having Trenchard as Commissioner was that he didn't like coppers. He couldn't bleedin' stand them. He considered we wasn't good enough, so he decided to give us an officer class. He accepted graduates straight from university and within a few years they filled most of the middle ranks. I've met some bloody good blokes in this job, blokes who could have gone right to the top, but they didn't – and why? Bloody Trenchard-Boys, that's why!' By this time his cigarette was just a tiny charred ember. To my utter astonishment he again raised his lighter. After two or three angry flicks, a pale yellow flame once more licked the scorched stub. He grimaced as the hairs of his nostrils seemed to singe. 'Him – bloody Jimmy-the-one – he's bloody typical of them all. He runs this nick without knowin' the first thing about the men under him. How could he? He's never been a proper copper. You can't learn this job at a college! You have to learn it out there – on the streets. This job's all about experience and common sense.' He stopped speaking for a moment, finally removing the burnt wisp from his mouth. He studied it for a second, and for one awful moment I thought he was about to relight it. Instead, and after due consideration, he returned it lovingly to its tin. 'Tell me,' he asked confidentially, 'have you ever seen a graduate with common sense? Well, have you?' he demanded.

At that precise moment I could not even remember seeing a graduate of any sort, dim or otherwise. He seemed to take my silence as disagreement. His voice rose an octave and he glared at me.

'I'll tell you what.' He deliberately and powerfully punched out each word, and he glared at me. 'I ain't seen a graduate yet that I'd send for a cut-loaf, never mind run a bloody police station!'

'We don't still have them, do we?' I asked, trying desperately to get back in with him. 'Trenchard-Boys, I mean.'

'The last of them came in in 1939 but it still takes thirty years to get the buggers through the system.' He sniffed and straightened his coat. 'Jimmy-the-one!' He vehemently spat out the name, together with a strand of tobacco that had, phoenix-like, survived the flames. 'C'mon, let's go for a walk.'

Once this barrier of distrust was removed, old George began to open up. Chief Inspector James Hall, alias Jimmy-the-one, Trenchard-Boy throughout, had been sent, George alleged, to clean up the manor. The majority of constables lived locally, and, with the popular East Street market less than two hundred yards from the station, it seemed that the lower ranks had become just a little too friendly with the traders.

East Street market of course did not consist only of stall-holders. It was a minefield of bookmakers, flypitchers (unlicensed traders) and street gamers. The market had run like this for over a century. It was certainly a little anarchic and sometimes even unlawful. Traders would use the pavement for their wares and cheerfully carry on selling after closing time (1 p.m. on Sundays). But this, after all, was the attraction of the market, this was what markets were all about. This was why thousands would flock there each Sunday morning. A place like the market was anathema to Jimmy's tidy mind. The stalls, he considered, should be in neat painted squares. The flypitchers, he decreed, must go, together with the crown-and-anchor men, the street entertainers and selling after hours. The traders did not like this; the street gamers did not like this; and the coppers did not like this. Now Jimmy was in fact a fair-minded and extremely intelligent man. Unfortunately he could never understand an area like Southwark. In Hampstead or Belgravia, he would have been marvellous. In East Street he was a calamity. He thought it was Chicago.

Some six months after I arrived at Carter Street, Chief Inspector James Hall was promoted and transferred.

'It'll take the market years to recover from 'im,' complained a mournful old linoleum-seller to me. As a local boy I sadly agreed.

Five days later, on a bright Sunday morning, I threaded my way throught the dense market crowd. Flypitchers abounded, boxes and baskets were everywhere, and a three-piece band played out of tune on a street corner. The only thing lacking was bunting across the road. It was less than a week since Jimmy had gone – and it was already as if he had never arrived in the first place!

'All right, Ginger-boy?' called the lino-man, cheerfully waving a golden-yellow bottle in my direction. ''Ave a drink, son. It's business as usual!'

3. 'No cause for police action'

I was not sure quite what I expected of becoming a policeman. There would be cops-an'-robbers to be played, no doubt, with breathtaking nick-of-time appearances. Other than that I had no set idea of what a policeman did. This was probably just as well because it turned out that three-quarters of our time on the Carter Street manor was taken up with domestic disputes. Easier divorce and wider recognition of women's rights mean these incidents are nowhere near as numerous today. Until the fifties, however, few working-class couples were divorced. No matter how disastrous the marriage, they would remain together. This, plus an acute housing shortage, caused distress to thousands of women. Wife-beating was almost a cottage industry, and many women seemed quite prepared to accept it as part and parcel of married life. They would sometimes complain when violence became a little too excessive, but by the next day they had shrugged it off. Many wives came to accept a lifetime of this cruelty.

'Never get involved in husband-and-wife disputes, son,' I was told. 'It'll always go bent on you in the end.'

Sadly, this was right. New young recruits would leap into these domestic affrays and arrest the husband, yet they never once won such a case at court. The wife, who the previous night would have pulled any rope that would hang her spouse, would always change her story in front of the magistrate the next morning. The inevitable result was that the young constable would have no evidence: the wife was usually the entire case, so without her there was nothing. After this had happened to a recruit a couple of times, he did tend to become reticent in his marital intrusions.

It was with this advice in mind that I attended my first domestic assault. A neighbour had reported hearing screams coming from the fourth floor of Seaton House, a small council block close by the Elephant and Castle. I called at number 37 and the door was eventually opened by a frail dyed-blonde with a thick, cut lip. She looked a sad little creature in her shapeless winceyette nightdress. She led me into the flat and all I could see were kids, who seemed to be everywhere. I counted at least seven, all, even though it was barely forty minutes to midnight, wide awake and lively.

Her husband had apparently returned from the public house and found her asleep. Desiring his conjugal rights, he had expected her to be glamorous and awaiting his drunken passion. The poor girl, looking as if a fortnight's sleep would have done no harm at all, understandably spurned his advances. Not accepting this, he had beaten her to the floor and, for good measure, dragged the children from their beds. He had then wandered out of the flat. The children appeared to be quite used to this treatment and not to mind in the least. Three of them chattily shared a comic on the settee while two others asked if they could switch on the late-night radio.

'It's the third time this week, mate,' she sighed, in response to my questioning. 'You see I've not been very well, I've been passing blood and such like and he don't seem to understand.'

She was also worried that her screams had disturbed the neighbours and was obviously unhappy about my presence. 'We'll get notice to quit at this rate,' she said sadly, shaking her head.

I bathed her cuts under the kitchen tap but she could scarcely conceal her anxiety for me to depart. 'I don't want no trouble, mate. It'll be all right, you'll see,' she kept repeating.

She made sure that all the children returned to their beds and showed me impatiently to the door.

'Are you sure that you feel safe enough for me to leave?' I asked.

'Yeh, I'm fine, mate, I'm fine. But don't make a noise as you go down the stairs, will you? I don't want all the neighbours upset again.'

I left the block with a sense of inadequacy and wondering just what else I might have done. I walked down towards the Elephant and Castle where I intended to ring the station from a police telephone post. As I neared the post I could see the warning-light flashing its yellow sign. Just before I reached it, a small black saloon car eased into the kerb and an inspector from neighbouring Kennington police station emerged. We shared this post with both Kennington and Southwark police stations and it was the only means that the station had to keep in touch with us once we were on the street. I saluted him and held back while he spoke into the handset.

'Have you just been to a disturbance in Seaton House, son?'

'Yessir.'

'Well, you can go back again. Apparently a neighbour's just phoned and the old man has returned home and the wife is screaming the place down.'

I sighed and turned away from him.

'Hang on. Have you ever dealt with a family dispute before?'

'No, sir. My first one.'

'What's it about?'

I quickly recounted the events to him.

'McGing you say the name is?'

I nodded.

'Blonde girl, umpteen kids?'

I nodded again.

'I know 'em well! Used to live on our manor. You gonna have to do something about him, son, he'll be knocking her about all night otherwise.'

'Well, what can I do? She doesn't want to know about any police action.'

'No, of course she don't, but I know how to deal with that monkey. Come on, I'll give you a lift round there. I might even look in meself.'

A few minutes later I once more stepped over the threshold of number 37. This time I was accompanied.

'Oh, hullo, Mr Bowyer,' exclaimed the blonde. 'What're you doin' here? I didn't think this was your manor.'

If she had looked bad previously, she looked awful now. Her nightdress was torn and her bare, hollow right shoulder was covered with small abrasions that led down to her tiny breast.

'Hullo, May,' said the inspector. 'Where is he?'

'He's gone, Mr Bowyer,' she said quietly. 'But if you was to see him, d'you think you could have a word with him? I don't know how much more of this I can take. I've lost two stone in as many months.'

'Are you sure you won't charge him, May? You should, you know. He's going to kill you one way or the other.'

'No, it's all right, Mr Bowyer, you just have a word with him, eh?'

Once more the children were returned to bed and once more I began to descend the staircase.

'You'd never believe she was a real beauty up until a year or two ago, would you?' the inspector asked.

'I certainly wouldn't.'

'How old d'you think she is?'

I guessed by the nature of the question that she was far younger than she appeared. I thought she looked all of forty-two. 'Late thirties?' I obliged.

'Twenty-eight,' he muttered. 'Twenty-eight, nine kids and a miscarriage. At least that was at the last count. God only knows what it is now. If she'd been my daughter I'd have killed him long ago.'

The dim staircase lights cut off automatically at midnight

so we felt our way down with some difficulty.

'Listen!' he commanded. 'There's someone coming up. Have you a torch?'

'Well, yes, but it doesn't work.' Other than a slight 'tch' he showed no surprise at this, probably because eighty per cent of the force torches never worked.

'I bet it's him, the bastard!' He pulled me back into a recessed doorway just before a large beer-bellied figure panted by.

'It's him right enough,' he whispered. 'Be quiet and we'll follow him up the stairs.'

He held me back with his arm until the figure was at least two flights ahead of us. 'Come on,' he instructed, tugging at my sleeve.

The man had soon reached number 37 and immediately began to pound the door with his fists. A thin streak of light filtered through the frosted glass partition above the door.

'C'mon, you lazy cow, open up.'

Although we could hear her voice, we were too far away to decipher the exact words. They appeared to be about both ourselves and the neighbours.

'I don't give a fuck about them *or* the police. Open this bloody door!'

Again we heard her implorings.

'If you don't open this fucking door, May, I'll swing for you, I will, I promise.'

'You could just about be right there, Danny,' interrupted the inspector.

The man wheeled around. 'Mr Bowyer!' he exclaimed. His mood changed instantly and he began to back away. 'Er, how are yer, Mr Bowyer?'

The inspector sadly shook his head and advanced upon the now frightened husband. 'Oh Danny, oh Danny, you fat, evil bastard. What *have* you done to that poor girl? There's almost nothing left of her.'

'Yeah, she's had a bit of a chill, like,' agreed the man. 'But she's fine really.'

By this time the man had backed out of the faint light and into the darkness at the side of the door. I saw no more than the slightest of moves but the cry, followed by the crash, told me it was a powerful one.

'Okay, May, you can open up now,' said the inspector to the still closed door.

A bolt was slid and a terrified, tearful wisp shivered half-naked in the chill air.

'He's all right, is he, Mr Bowyer?' she asked anxiously as she clutched her own shoulders with crossed arms.

'I hope not,' muttered the inspector almost to himself. 'Let's have a bit of light out here and we'll soon see.'

She swung back the door wide and the dingy light from the passageway revealed a semi-conscious bulk sprawling on the concrete floor.

I had observed the entire proceedings as detached as if I had been watching a film. This had never happened at training school. A short command from the inspector broke the spell: 'Come on, son, give us a hand. He's bloody heavy!'

We half-carried, half-dragged the moaning Daniel into the flat and dumped him on to a rumpled bed. There was no light in the bedroom, only an empty electric socket hanging bulbless from the ceiling. Yet again we had to make do with the forty-watt passageway light.

'Haven't you got a bulb for this room, May?' asked the inspector irritably. 'You need to be a bloody bat to live here.'

'I'll take the one from the passage,' said May as she scuttled away with a chair.

Seconds later we were again plunged into darkness as our only illumination was removed. I soon felt the bed shake as she clambered up on to it and turned the hot bulb into the socket. A faint click followed and each corner of the room became just about visible. The bedding was tatty and frayed and so were the curtains. A tiny faded bedside mat was the only covering on the unpainted floorboards.

There was no cupboard or wardrobe in the room, but an assortment of clothing lay piled upon the armchairs. These chairs had sustained such wear that the upholstery had worn smooth. Every aspect of that room showed signs of poverty. Yet it was absolutely spotless. Even in that ridiculous light it looked clean.

'Come on, Dan, wake up,' pleaded May as she knelt on the mattress and peered anxiously into his face.

As she leaned forward her nightdress gaped and I could see for the first time the full extent of her injuries. I gestured to the inspector and he closed his eyes in resignation.

'What's that, May?' he gently asked, pointing to her torso.

She quickly pulled the garment around her. 'It's just a bruise, Mr Bowyer, only a bruise.'

'May, they are not bruises, love, are they?'

She made no reply but dropped her gaze to the bed.

'Bruises don't go in neatly curved patterns, May, do they?'

She remained silent.

'Teeth marks do, though, don't they, May?'

I thought she would remain silent but she suddenly knelt upright and pulled open the whole upper part of the nightgown. Not only was she covered in bites, but at least three of them were still trickling blood. Blood seemed to be in fashion – a fair quantity of it was coming from Daniel McGing's lip.

'When did he bite you, May, the first or second time?'

'The second time, Mr Bowyer. It hurt a bit, that was why I screamed.' She smiled wryly. 'There's not as much of me as there used to be, you know.'

Tight and fleeting though her smile had been, for a split second I had seen a glimpse of her former beauty.

Danny was now wide awake and sobering fast. He had never been fully drunk but just enough to be thoroughly obnoxious. The inspector then sat on the bed and pulled

40

him up to a sitting position by his shirt front.

'Listen, you pig, you've been getting away with this for years for no other reason than she stupidly sticks by you and refuses to charge. But when you've finally killed her, as you certainly will, there'll be no "refused-to-charge" then. You'll be up those steps at the Bailey before you know where you are. When that day comes, you had better pray that I have nothing to do with the case.' With that he threw the now weeping Daniel back on to the pillow.

'Oh Danny, Danny,' cried May as she bent forward and cradled his great greasy head to her pathetic body. 'I'm really sorry, Dan, honest I am. It wasn't my fault, though. I didn't call them. It was the neighbours.'

'Nosey bastards all of 'em,' whined the tearful Daniel. 'It's a pity they've got nothing better to do.'

May looked sadly up at the inspector. 'He'll be all right now, Mr Bowyer, honest he will. Now that you've had a word with him, he'll be as good as gold.'

'May, you're a fool.'

'No, straight up, Mr Bowyer, he will. You see, well, he gets a bit frustrated because –' she shrugged helplessly – 'I'm having a bad time with me next and he thinks . . .'

'May!' The inspector threw his head back in disbelief. 'You're never expecting *again*, surely?'

She appeared to fight for words for a few moments as she stroked the blubbering head at her yielding but inadequate breast. 'Well, Danny likes to have kids around him and –' She looked hauntedly around the room as if searching for something good to say about him. 'Well, he's a good father really.'

'Good father! If it hadn't been for you those kids would have all been in care years ago and you know it.'

She made no reply to this but just dropped her head to Daniel's as the tears welled up in her eyes.

The inspector shook his head, leaned forward for a second and fondly ruffled her dyed locks. He then turned his attention to me.

'Come on, son, we have no further function here. We'll see ourselves out, May. Goodnight,' he called.

'Goodnight, Mr Bowyer, and thanks. Goodnight to you too, mate. I'm sorry that you had to come back.'

'That's okay, May,' I responded. 'Don't let it worry you. Goodnight.'

'Mister,' came the sleepy call from the living-room, 'we've finished all our comics. Can we go back to bed now?' In all the trauma we had forgotten the children!

'Yes, of course, off you go,' said the inspector. 'Your dad is all right now,' he assured them.

'Did you knock 'im out, mister?' asked a little pyjama-clad girl.

'Er – well, no, he slipped over and cut his lip.'

'Tony said that you knocked 'im out. Tony said that you used to knock 'im out when we lived in the other 'ouse, too.'

'Well, your dad does fall about quite a bit, you know.'

'Yeh, I know,' agreed the child. 'When dad 'urts me mum the next time, will you come round and knock 'im out again?'

'You hop into bed now.'

'Will you, mister? Will you? Tony said that dad is always a lot better after you've knocked 'im out.'

'We'll see. Now off to bed. Goodnight.'

'G'night, mister; g'night, mate.'

It appeared that I was everyone's mate that night, as at least six little voices echoed that farewell.

As we made our way once again down the inhospitable stairs, I wondered how I would report the incident. I assumed it would be down to me because although the Inspector had taken charge, I had been the first on the scene and anyway it was my manor. I thought back to all those set-pieces and stock sayings that I had learned at training school. 'What has happened here, sir, please?' 'Did anyone see what happened?' 'Do you wish to take out a summons for assault?' They had never told me about putting kids to bed after knocking out their father.

'Er, excuse me, sir,' I finally asked, 'but how do I report it?'

'You don't.'

'But they told us at training school that we had to report everything.'

'You do that, son, and you will never stop writing.'

'Well, what shall I show as a "result" on the record of the emergency call at the police station?'

'Simply show "husband-and-wife dispute", then add "no cause for police action". If you start reporting every husband-and-wife dispute the whole bloody administrative system will grind to a halt.'

He was right, of course. In husband-and-wife disputes we were not policemen at all, we were referees. In many cases we were not even that. The blunt sentence, 'Don't tell me how to run my marriage, son, I've got four kids older than you,' takes a great deal of answering. All over the city these daily battles between spouses would ignite. I soon learnt – we all learnt – that *officially* they never took place at all. How could they have done? They were never reported. Not even the knock-outs.

'What happened at number 37, Cole?'

'Nothing, sarge, nothing at all. It was a husband-and-wife dispute. "No cause for police action".'

4. The outing

Although I had soon begun to enjoy my police work, morale in general at the station was undoubtedly low. This state of affairs was to change within weeks, however, as the new chief inspector made his presence felt. And what a presence! It was even more striking than Jay-Oh-Dee's! Chief Inspector Samuel Parry was a huge man whose voice had never lost its soft Fenland burr. With his ruddy complexion and thick silvery hair, he looked more like a successful farmer than a police officer. He was meticulously smart and gave out an air of detached authority. He had worked his way steadily up through the ranks and was greatly respected by all. Sam not only *looked* a guv'nor, he *was* a guv'nor! This was best illustrated in an incident that took place a few months after he arrived.

The Elephant Club was an illegal drinking-den that had become a haven for half the cut-throats and villains in south London. We raided it soon after midnight on Friday with just a dozen coppers and an inspector. The clientele sitting at the bar had collectively served some two hundred years' imprisonment between them. The rest, who were sitting at tables, probably took the score to a thousand. It looked like the Black Museum. There were murderers, robbers and grievous bodily harmers; plus pimps, ponces and pushers. To make matters doubly worse, their molls and dolls were with them. Also, just as an additional hazard, there were more weapons in the place than in the whole of the Woolwich Arsenal. It was therefore no exaggeration to say that the raid had been sadly underpoliced and woefully underplanned. Nor was it an exaggeration to say that I for one was scared witless.

As the inspector tried vainly to make himself heard, the resentful crowd became quite threatening. Suddenly, and seemingly out of nowhere, Sam Parry appeared in the doorway. He looked all of fifteen feet tall. 'B-e-e qui-ert!' he boomed. And everyone was! It was utter and complete silence. Not a soul moved. 'I want you to give your names and addresses to the officers here,' he gestured generally in our direction. 'And if no offences are disclosed, you will be allowed to go home peacefully – *peacefully*, mark you!' he reminded.

And so peacefully it was. The place never opened again in all the years Sam was at Carter Street.

Sam Parry, then, was like a breath of fresh air to us. He wasn't totally flawless, though – he could be an unforgiving man. He forgot very little. Once, when he requested some improvements in the single men's sleeping quarters, he was obliged to conduct a surveyor around the premises. During this tour, the pair entered the canteen where PC Alan Thomas sat playing cards with myself and Jimmy Davenport. Alan had overstayed his mealbreak by some fifteen minutes and should have been out on the streets. Sam appeared not to notice and Alan optimistically believed he had not been seen – a particularly foolish assumption on his part, for Sam missed nothing. Six weeks later, through an incredible piece of intuitive police work, Alan was responsible for the arrest of a whole team of lorry hijackers. Thousands of pounds were involved, at a time when a working man's wages were ten pounds a week. The DI (detective inspector) was delighted. The captured team had been well 'at it' and scores of crimes were cleared up. He suggested to Sam that Alan should be recommended for an award.

'I don't think so,' said Sam matter-of-factly. 'He owes me that.' As far as Sam was concerned the slate was now clean.

Meanwhile, I was finding one great problem in my transition to becoming a policeman. The difficulty was with the speed of my stroll. Slow walking had always tired me. Even when learning beats I had consistently collided with my colleagues. I had therefore been itching to get out on my own, so I could speed up my pace.

On my first morning of early-turn, I had been posted to number three beat. This beat was the smallest on the manor and covered little more than half of the market.

Dead on six o'clock, I left the station and crossed the Walworth Road on to my beat. There I set off at a natural pace and eventually completed the first circuit of my patch for that day.

I glanced up indifferently at the pawnbroker's clock and made a mental note that it had stopped. Checking the time with my own wristwatch, I was surprised to find that it, too, had stopped, strangely enough at the same time. Why, I wondered, should both timepieces stop at 6.20 a.m.? Was there perhaps some strong magnetic pull, generated by the now bright sun and peculiar to the Walworth Road? I soon realized that both timepieces showed 6.20 a.m. purely because it *was* 6.20 a.m. I had been around the entire perimeter of my territory in twenty minutes! I still had another seven hours and forty minutes to go!

'Slow down, sunshine!' called a cheery blonde office-cleaner from the nearby bus-stop. 'You won't last the bleedin' day!'

Within a week I could circuit number three beat in just under fifty minutes. Within a year, by chatting to the paper-seller, lavatory attendant and Betty in the baker's, I had got it up to three hours. Within two years and at weekends when all of the stallholders were in place, I could not manage it in a whole day!

Even though the three months at Peel House were now well behind us, recruits were required to attend a weekly instruction class. This usually took place on a Wednesday. The aim, they told us, was to maintain that finely honed legal edge we had diligently acquired at the training school. The only acceptable excuse for missing these hated classes was a court appearance. As a result, local law-breaking appeared to rise dramatically on the day before the classes were held: the number of arrests on that day would increase by some twenty per cent.

'Why this regular Tuesday crime wave?' Scotland Yard would ask.

The answer was, of course, that there were some fifteen recruits wandering the division, desperately seeking the only known alternative to an instruction class on Wednesday – nick someone Tuesday. That local barrow-boy who had merely been *summoned* for illegal trading on Monday found himself *arrested* for obstruction the following day. The financial penalties were the same – ten bob with time to pay – but that short court appearance had reprieved the young officer from three hours of dreaded revision, plus a whole evening's homework.

When, after eight months, the classes were changed to Fridays, the indignation this caused among the flypitchers was astonishing.

''Ere! You can't nick me,' they would complain. 'It ain't Tuesday!'

These teething troubles aside, I found my acceptance as a recruit was gradually made easier by my participation in police sport, plus a keenness on almost any form of station outing. I have, for example, always loved a coach trip to the races. These were extremely popular in the fifties. A strange, archaic rule, however, governs all forms of police off-duty behaviour: discipline regulations require that whenever a body of men leave a station for any organized social function, they must have a chaperon! No outing is allowed without one. It matters not that the same men, or women, are considered adult enough to deal with any public disorder prior to the trip. Once they set foot on a coach in an off-duty capacity, then the chaperon must always be present. This officially appointed overseer is

47

usually an inspector. It is hoped that he too will be travelling purely in the role of an off-duty policeman. It is then further hoped that he will combine this role with the responsibility of his rank and not, for example, urinate out of the coach window. Of course, it then becomes his function to make sure that nobody else does either. This can sometimes put temptation where none would normally exist. It would not be the first coach load of overhappy coppers that was supervised by an unpopular inspector. The singing of lewd songs through open windows in traffic jams could, under such circumstances, become something of an obligation.

On the whole, though, the chaperons are on the trip for no other reason than that they wish to be there. In such cases, the relationship with the lower ranks is particularly harmonious and the men lean over backwards to be fair. Just occasionally, however, he can suffer from a little too much help. Take an early outing to Brighton, for example.

Thirty-six men left the station on a heat-hazed morning for Brighton races. A pleasant enough day had been spent on the course, and soon after 5 p.m. the coach returned to take us on into the town for a meal. Later that evening, having wined and dined to reasonable excess, we gradually assembled on our coach.

'Okay, driver, off we go,' yelled a helpful voice from the back seat.

'Whoa! Just a minute,' interrupted Inspector Andrews, sensibly checking his list. 'Let's make sure we're all here first.'

He pointed a quivering stubby finger at each occupant and at the same time beat out a rapid count. 'Thirty-four . . . thirty-five . . . thirty-six.' He seemed finally satisfied. 'Yes, that's all right now, driver. Whenever you're ready!'

'You never counted yourself, guv',' commented a sleepy voice from the second row back.

'Eh? Oh, I'm sure I did. Anyway the numbers work out right. Thirty-six of us out and thirty-six back.'

'But with you that comes to thirty-seven,' persisted the voice.

Andrews sighed and with slow deliberation began again. This time he made great play of first prodding himself. 'One, right?' He looked questioningly at the voice.

The voice nodded dutifully back.

'Two . . .' Boozy helpers then began to assist him with the count. 'Thirty-five . . . thirty-six . . . oh bloody hell! Thirty-seven!'

'Told yer!'

Again he studied his list.

'I don't know him, guv'.' George Rearsden was pointing to one of several sleepers on the back seat. 'That bloke curled up there at the end. I've never seen him before.'

Our attention was collectively drawn to a slim man of some fifty-five years, sound asleep on one end of the back seat.

'Does *anyone* know him?' asked the inspector anxiously.

Some of the men had brought friends on the trip and we thought it could possibly be one of these. We woke up all the other sleepers – some were quite irritable – but no claimant for the mysterious stranger presented himself.

'Wake him up, find out who he is,' said Andrews. 'He's obviously nothing to do with anyone here.'

The bleary-eyed stowaway eventually blinked at the sea of enquiring faces and made his explanation with Guinness-laden breath. 'I missed me coach 'ome, guv'nor. I thought I'd get a lift on the next coach I saw. I climbed in and must of dropped off.'

'Well, where d'you live?' asked Andrews. Before the question could be answered, the newcomer dropped his head once more into instant sleep. 'Come on, we haven't got all night,' the inspector continued. 'Search him.'

During the search, the man roused and muttered that his name was Charlie Watkins and he lived in Battersea. His driving licence bore this out and it was agreed we would make a detour on our return to London. Our driver was not too happy about this. He complained that whereas he would have avoided most of the traffic after Croydon, a trip to Battersea would put ten miles on the journey, to say nothing of an hour on the time. No one, however, is as saintly or self-righteous as a collection of half-drunks hell-bent on doing a favour for another inebriate. Battersea, then, it was most definitely going to be and the driver could stuff himself. With a bad-tempered crashing of gears, the coach leapt forward on the two-hour trip to south-west London.

There was one thing to be said for Charlie, he could sleep. He snored louder than the diesel. Finally, our coach turned into a quiet little street off Battersea Park Road. We jerked to a halt outside number 47. Most of us passengers, fired with the spirit of comradeship, decided to escort our new friend safely to his door. We clustered three-deep around the little terraced house as Inspector Andrews knocked loudly. A pretty, fair-haired girl of about twenty opened the door. What was obviously a customary smile vanished the instant she laid eyes on Charlie.

'Dad! Whatever's the matter?' she exclaimed anxiously.

A motley of reassurance came from our escorting group: 'Don't you worry, sweetheart, we've looked after him,' 'He's all right, love, your old dad's been safe with us,' 'It's been a pleasure to have him, darling,' to list but three.

'But what's the matter?' she persisted. 'What exactly has happened?'

Andrews called for order from the ramblings of the group and took it upon himself to explain to the girl the precise nature of events.

'So you see, miss,' he concluded, 'we decided to bring him home all safe and sound, like. I mean we couldn't just leave him there, now could we?'

'Well, I can't see why not,' said the girl with a deep sigh. 'He left here this morning to go to Brighton for a week's holiday.'

'That's right,' agreed Charlie, losing his enthusiasm for

his benefactors. 'And where's me suitcase, eh? Tell me that!'

The cheerful reassurances all vanished, as twenty gallant men climbed back on to the coach and decided that Inspector Andrews was just the man for such a situation. Well, after all, he was the chaperon, wasn't he?

5. Decorators, undertakers and Avon ladies

Although I was settling down well in my work, the same could not be said for my private life. Our housing problem was going from bad to worse. Having moved into a flat just a few months earlier, we had discovered that the 'landlady' who had sublet to us had absolutely no authority to do so. We were therefore under notice to quit. This was complicated by the fact that she had insisted on a year's rent in advance. With eight months still in credit and no place to move into, we decided to stay put.

This was a sensible idea in theory but a nightmare in practice. The biggest of the many problems this posed was the hygienic standards of our landlady. She had none. There was, for example, no bathroom in the house and we shared the only lavatory with her and her lodger. She would frequently hold parties for semi-vagrants and it was by no means unusual for me to return home after night-duty and find fourteen empty beer-crates stacked behind the front door. The vomit-strewn lavatory pan would look like an open sewer and the smell was indescribable. We had two bottles of Air-wick (a proprietary air-freshener at the time) standing on permanent duty on the staircase, fighting a sad losing battle.

After some months of this, I applied to see the Metropolitan Police Welfare Officer, who was a retired naval commander. He was based at Scotland Yard and spoke mainly in clichés.

'We all have our little housing problems, you know,' he pointed out. 'You see,' he went on, 'I know that you would like me to give you priority for police accommodation, yes?'

I had to admit that was the purpose of my visit.

'Well, I can't, I'm afraid. You see, it would be a precedent. If I were to obtain accommodation for you, well we'd have every Tom, Dick and Harry leaping on the bandwagon purely to occupy a flat.'

'So what do I do?'

'Grin and bear it, lad, grin and bear it,' he cliché'd. 'These things are sent to try us and they have a habit of sorting themselves out in due course.'

'Trenchard's idea,' angrily muttered George Rearsden the following day as I confided my worries to him.

'What was?' I asked, not quite understanding why Trenchard should wish to keep me out of police accommodation.

'Having senile old sailors as welfare officers. It was a wonder he didn't tell you to sling a bloody hammock under a tree!'

I was beginning to find myself disliking Trenchard as much as George did. To be fair to the Commander, though, he was proved right. Things did sort themselves out in due course. Seven *years* of due course to be exact. I never bothered to visit him again, although I did make a mental note to apply for a naval welfare job once I had left the force.

Private problems aside, my first two years in the police passed with a surprising speed. The station was by then quite a happy one. Soon after I completed my two-year probationary period, I received a very welcome windfall. A national train strike had been declared and lasted for seventeen days. With far fewer cars on the road than today, people piled on to anything that moved. Lorries, vans and horse and carts. Roads in south-east London were horrendous. For every day of the dispute, street constables were obliged to work a twelve- to fourteen-hour day, weekends included. The strike, however, was by no means an ill wind. Those two and a half weeks of compulsory overtime enabled Joan and me to buy two new armchairs and a secondhand gas stove.

To assist our station in its constabulary labours, twenty-five members of the East Sussex Police Force were seconded to us for the duration of the strike. These men had mainly policed the small villages and towns on the Kent-Sussex border. Many of them found the rough-and-tumble of inner-city life a fascinating contrast. The biggest single difference between the two forces was in the question of discipline. In comparison to theirs we had none.

'It'll take me six months to get this lot back to normal once we leave here,' complained the inspector in charge of them.

I must admit they were certainly smarter and about three inches taller than we were, and they tended to take the job more seriously. On the whole they seemed to enjoy their stay, although they never really came to terms with the informality of the London force.

Probably because I welcomed the money, I enjoyed the strike. The same could not be said for all my colleagues. For Peter Ward it was the last straw. We had spent a wet Tuesday morning on the multiple traffic point at Kennington Oval. Four of us had tried to resolve some sort of system. We had not been too successful; we were really beaten before we had started by the sheer volume of traffic. Our attitude was that if we could not speed it up, then at least we would try to be fair. We therefore gave each line of vehicles an equal-time run across the junctions.

One serious disadvantage for any copper on an Oval traffic point, is its very location. Almost half of all vehicles entering central London from the south, must pass across its junctions. Not only that but it soon became obvious that three-quarters of all very senior police officers and Whitehall dignitaries passed through each morning on their way to work. Each in turn pointed out to the sweating, soaked and beleaguered copper that he was not handling the traffic at all well. Matters reached a head when a testy Assistant Commissioner finally chugged up to Peter's section.

'Who,' demanded the frustrated demi-god, 'is in charge here this morning?'

Peter looked at him ruefully for a moment then slowly pulled off his traffic gauntlets and thrust them into the open car window. 'Every effer,' snapped the weary Peter. With that he spun on his heels and walked briskly back to the station where he resigned.

Peter's action was certainly unusual even by Met standards. PCs as a general rule tend not to speak frankly to Assistant Commissioners. On the other hand, its effect on our East Sussex counterparts was astonishing. They did not stop discussing it for days. At one time I thought he would have to sign autographs.

Like all good things the strike ended and my wages reverted to their customary low. PCs at that time had enormous difficulty in making ends meet, so most married men had part-time jobs. This was in strict contravention of the service regulation that began, 'Whole time to police service . . .' Men would parade for duty with plaster in their hair, paint on their fingers and horse-dung on their boots. My own relief alone amassed two lorry drivers, three bakers, a joiner, a plumber, four painters, two stable hands and an undertaker, albeit in a part-time capacity. One group of enterprising constables even had their own trade-name on a display board which they would erect outside any house where they worked.

Many embarrassing situations arose from these illegal activities. There was the publican, for example, who complained that two constabulary stalwarts had papered his entire saloon bar with ludicrously expensive wallpaper but had hung it upside down.

There was also the Walworth vicar who, after having a particularly thick-piled carpet laid, contacted a 'skilled carpenter and joiner' whose card was displayed in a local newsagents. The task was simple enough, half-inch from the bottom of six interior and two exterior doors. The skilled carpenter, alias PC 921 Woodfull, removed all the doors and laid them out on the back lawn, where he smoothly trimmed them in the late summer sunshine. It would have been an impressively neat job, too, had he not taken the half-inch from the *top* of each door. A thick-piled carpet and eight doors with a gap at the wrong end does nothing at all for draughts. Poor Jack Woodfull was at first inconsolable, and the vicar wasn't too happy either! However, Jack perked up appreciably when he heard that Paddy Kennedy had lost three fingertips on a grocer's bacon-slicer. There is nothing quite like someone else's disaster to help you over your own.

Other officers earned money in different fields. One was a selling-agent from a catalogue, while another bred budgies. A year or two later, one balding middle-aged giant became the station's 'Avon lady'. He would think nothing of opening his sample-case in a crowded canteen and extolling the virtues of a delicate eye-liner. 'It'd suit your missus a treat,' was his entire sales vocabulary.

Although these part-time jobs were rife – I, for instance, decorated, drove a delivery van for a market shop and sold electric blankets at Christmas – the hierarchy made determined efforts to stamp them out. One young PC, while facing a difficult promotion interview board, mentioned he was a soccer referee.

'D'you get paid?' they asked him.

'Fifteen and sixpence,' he replied.

'Have you declared it?'

'Declared it?' asked the puzzled young constable.

'Yes, declared it – declared it!' they insisted. 'It's another source of income and you are only allowed to accept it if you get permission.'

'But it costs me half a quid to get there in the first place,' he protested.

At this the board went into a huddle and eventually came to the grudging conclusion that he could keep the extra five and sixpence after all. He thanked them politely and praised his lucky stars he had made no mention of his insurance round.

By the mid-fifties, I had completed my probationary period. I was then free to apply for one of the force's specialized departments, the obvious one being the CID. This move would, I felt, need careful thought. The big difference between the CID and the uniformed branch was that they were simply not compatible. They were just two completely separate ways of life. Old coppers would scathingly refer to the CID as the 'Brains Department'. Many of them had a talent to make those two words sound like the ultimate insult. I had the feeling right from my earliest days that the attitude of the uniformed branch was basically one of envy. This negative attitude was not helped by the CID themselves, for many detectives acted as if they *were* the superior department.

Working in the CID is undoubtedly the more glamorous job, and detectives with their extra freedom and financial allowances were considerably better off than us. One of the worst things that can happen to a detective is to be returned to a uniform. It is consistently denied that this is meant as a punishment. Yet never in the history of the force has any uniformed copper been sentenced to become a detective.

At Carter Street this division was perpetuated even into the canteen. This facility was situated in the basement and consisted of just two small rooms. The CID used one and the uniformed branch the other. It was amid this atmosphere of mistrust and jealousy that I, as a two-year recruit, had to decide whether to fight or join them. To assist this decision, a week's attachment to the department was allowed. This was fine up to a point, but during my attachment only one detective ever took me out. For most of the week I was ignored and just sat boredly around the office or made the tea.

The detective who took it upon himself to show me at least some of the ropes was an eccentric gentleman named Bill Jay. Bill possessed a huge old Humber motor car and a dirty-white male dog named Pansy. He thought the world of both. He would bring Pansy to work each day and, provided the weather was not too hot, would kennel the dog outside the station in his motor car. I have no idea what he fed the creature, but to ride in that car was a torture. It absolutely reeked. Up to a point policemen get used to oppressive smells, but Pansy really took some beating, he was so incredibly persistent. At forty miles an hour with all four windows open, the smell was hateful. With them all closed I felt suicidal. Bill daily sported a fresh flower buttonhole, yet no rose could ever compete with Pansy. To be fair to Bill, he never seemed to notice the smell. The only time he even vaguely acknowledged the presence of pollution was the first day I climbed into the passenger seat.

'Drop the window down a mite if you're warm,' he sang out. 'Pansy'd welcome a breeze, wouldn't you, boy?' The animal showed an objectionable gratitude by leaping on to my lap. 'He's taken to you, Ginger-boy,' Bill said marvellingly. 'He don't do *that* to everyone.'

In addition to his buttonhole, Bill wore a black homburg hat and carried a rolled umbrella. In spite of these adornments, he always managed to look like the council tip. Pansy's hairs of course did little to help. Some days Bill seemed to have more of them than did the dog. He was also one of those unfortunate people who looked worse the longer you looked at them. His long hair curled up at the nape of his neck and his mousey moustache would hang limp. His suit, though of good cut, had not seen a cleaner since the day of its purchase. A sparkling Guards tie was overshadowed by a frayed collar, and, finally, there was his hat. Again I would think not cheap, but it had spent too much time in Pansy's proximity. In fact it looked like the dog had slept in it. Knowing both Bill and Pansy, I would also surmise that he had.

In the four years that Bill was at the station, come rain or shine, I never once saw his brolly unfurled. In fact there was only his word for it that it was an umbrella at all. He swung, pointed, gestured and punctuated with it. Once, while on our way to Lambeth Court, two chunky navvies were digging up the road. One, with his back to us, was bent double and straining to extract a length of piping from the layers of tight-packed concrete. His feet were placed firmly astride and his short stocky legs filled every inch of his brown corded trousers. Everything about the man's action implied power. There was so much I felt something was about to explode. Either the pipe would break, the man would drop dead or perhaps his trousers would burst. In fact none of these happened. As we neared the man, Bill reached forward and, with the tip of his brolly, tapped the navvy lightly underneath his straining rectum.

'I say, you there,' murmured Bill casually. 'What is it you're doing?'

I prepared to duck.

With a loud grunt the man released the pipe and turned around panting. With great heaving shoulders he looked furiously at Bill and was, I am sure, all set to tear out his throat.

'What're you doing there?' repeated Bill, waving the umbrella generally around the hole.

'Who wants to know?' glared the navvy.

'I do,' answered Bill quietly. 'For all I know you could be stealing something.'

I looked around urgently for an escape. Then, to my complete astonishment, both workmen explained in great detail and with even more respect, how and why they were there. In fact on at least two occasions they even called him sir!

'Very well. Thank you very much,' said Bill. 'I just wanted to know. You can carry on now. Good morning.'

'G'morning, guv',' nodded both men respectfully, and

with that they resumed their battle with the hole.

As we walked on, Bill swung the brolly with an even jauntier air.

'Do you know,' I said incredulously, 'they didn't even ask who you were?'

'I know and I find that quite strange,' muttered Bill thoughtfully. 'And what's more they never do.'

As we approached the court, Bill asked me who else I had been out with that week. When I told him this had been the only offer, he showed no great surprise.

'You can't blame them. After all, they don't really know you.'

'Don't know me?' I exploded. 'I'm a bloody copper! I'm in the same force as they are yet it takes some of them all their time even to talk to me!'

'Yes, but be fair, you've shown no indication you wish to enter the department. As far as they are concerned you're just an interested spectator passing through. Taking you out can be quite time-consuming, you know,' he reproved.

'Thanks a lot!'

Bill replied with any easy laugh, then added: 'I didn't mean it quite like that. Look, how'd you like to come to the Old Bailey tomorrow? I've got a case there. You might find it interesting and it'd be good experience for you.'

'Thanks,' I murmured appreciatively as we climbed the steps of the court. 'I would like that very much.'

'Okay, be at the nick at nine o'clock sharp.'

We had reached the sturdy door that led to the back of the court and Bill raised his hand to knock for the gaoler. He paused in mid-movement, his fist still half-clenched.

'There is one other thing,' he said, with just a slight air of hesitation.

I looked at him questioningly.

He nodded generally at me then continued, 'Well, you will try to be a bit smart, won't you? I mean it *is* the Old Bailey after all.'

I must have gaped at him, and once I gathered my thoughts I was about to exclaim, 'You cheeky bastard!'

'Just make an effort – eh?' He smiled as he rapped loudly on the door.

The following morning, with gritted teeth, I took more than usual care about my appearance. I arrived at the station canteen soon after nine o'clock and promptly enquired about Bill.

'He's about,' I was told. 'Try the CID office.'

As I climbed the two flights I could clearly hear Bill's voice. It was not particularly loud but it had a surprising power of penetration. I opened the door and glanced in at the chaos that passes for an average busy CID office. This will usually look like the third week of a sit-in at the London School of Economics. Ours was no exception. The desks were littered with crime-sheets, local newspapers and unserviceable typewriters. A telephone rang here and there and three separate conversations were taking place across the room. Of Bill there was no sign.

At least there was no sign of the Bill Jay that *I* knew. Instead, sitting at his desk was a trimmed-moustached hair-cutted dandy, whom I had never before clapped eyes on.

'You're late,' he said, sliding back his chair and glancing pointedly at the wall-clock.

If I was impressed when he was sitting down, I was astonished once he had stood up. A sharp-cut, pin-stripe, three-piece suit rested upon him with an air of casual affluence. A winged collar and an inch of gold-linked cuff set the final seal upon the whole extravaganza.

'Look after him, Ginger,' called a harassed detective sergeant, clamping a meaty hand over a telephone mouthpiece. 'At twelve o'clock he turns back into a pumpkin.'

'C'mon, son,' called Bill, ignoring the remark. 'We've got a bus to catch.'

'A bus!' I echoed. 'Like that?'

'Well, I can't park my car near the Bailey – and I take it you won't pay for a taxi?'

'You take it right. I'm twenty-four years old and I have never even been in a taxi.'

I could not take my eyes from him, he was like a Jekyll and Hyde. I had never before seen such a transformation. In fact I was to see it many times over the next few years. The outfit was fondly known as 'Bill's Old Bailey suit'. God knows where he kept it when it was not in use. In a glass case in the Victoria and Albert, some said. Although Bill had to put up with many remarks and cat-calls, the suit never once finished on the losing side.

'Juries always believe toffs,' claimed Bill. 'It's an inbuilt inferiority complex they have.'

That day was no exception. A razor-slashing witness had 'gone bent' on the prosecution but it seemed not to matter as Bill took the oath and shone over the Bailey like a Beacon of Truth. Well, at least that was how he saw himself. Apparently the jury did too.

'Guilty, m'Lord,' said the foreman.

'Five years,' said m'Lord.

I revelled in the sheer theatre of that day. I had been to the Magistrates' Court many times and even occasionally to the Sessions (later to be known as Crown Courts), but to a policeman the Old Bailey is totally different. It is like the Palladium to a variety act, or Rome to a Catholic, or perhaps Wembley to Scunthorpe United. Yet even though I enjoyed my days with Bill, I also knew that the CID was not for me. Even if I could pass the educational requirements, I knew I would never make a detective. Whatever it was it took, I did not have it. Well, if I was not going to be a 'tec', what else could I do? Not a lot, I was beginning to realize.

6. It takes a worried man

Having finished my two-year probationary period, I was obliged to have my end-of-term interview with my Commander. Andrew Way was a magnificently rounded gentleman who would have measured the same regardless of which direction you started from. He was an enormous favourite with the men and, heaven forgive me and wash my mouth out for saying so – a Trenchard-Boy!

Being in charge of a police district will of course compel a Commander to assess his priorities. One of Andrew's greatest was the district football team. Whatever criticism this caused him to receive from other sources, he received none at all from me.

My interview with him came the day after I had represented the district in a cup-tie. It was a game that we had eventually lost because I tripped an opponent in the last two minutes of extra time and gave away a penalty. In addition to this, I was not overconfident of my character report. I was soon to hear the worst as I was finally shepherded into the great man's office.

'Ah, Cole! Do come in, I won't keep you a minute.'

With that he spent ten of them studying the report on the table in front of him. I stood to attention throughout and gazed apprehensively down at the same papers. Try as I might, from a standing position and upside-down I could only make out the occasional word. Those that I made out did not look good. Words like 'unpunctual' and 'too casual' can be read only too clearly from any angle.

'Hmmmmmm,' he finally murmured, raising his head and looking me straight in the eyes. 'There is one thing we must get perfectly clear right from the beginning, Cole.'

'Sir?'

'That was never a penalty in a million years!'

Now I may not be overbright but I know a life-line when I see one. 'Sir! You don't know how pleased I am to hear you say that. He fell over his feet, sir!'

'Unquestionably!' agreed Andrew. 'In my opinion the refereeing of that game left a great deal to be desired. Er – let me see, who was it now?'

'Sergeant Wilkinson, sir!' I had the name out almost before he had finished asking the question.

'Ah yes, so it was. Yes, I must have a word with Wilkinson. Good man normally. Anyway, other than the penalty, Cole, is there anything else that bothers you?'

I was tempted to ask for his help in a transfer to one of the few specialized departments. On second thoughts, however, I decided to quit while I was ahead.

'No, sir.'

'Nothing at all?'

'Well, only my living accommodation, sir.'

'Ah yes, I've read something about that.' He glanced down again at the file. 'Seen the welfare officer, have you?'

'Yes, sir.'

'Got it in hand, has he?'

'He's had it "in hand" for the past eighteen months, sir.'

'Yes, welfare officers tend to be a little like that. Gee him up, there's a good fellow. Anything else?'

'No, sir.'

'Very well, off you go and, er, just watch those tackles, eh?'

'Certainly, sir.'

'Good man. Congratulations on your confirmation. Tell the sergeant to send in the next man, will you?'

I believed there was a department somewhere that needed my experience but at the time I could not actually think of it. I decided therefore to continue on the beat for a while until I was struck with my vocation. I made no application for a move for another two years. This was not a deliberate ploy on my part, just indecision. In fact those years were not wasted at all. They were to stand me in good stead for the rest of my service; they were, I suppose, an investment.

Policing an area like Southwark in the days before personal radios and an abundance of men and vehicles tended to breed survivors. To be alone in a dark back-street alley at two in the morning, having just heard a window break, a door slam, or a muffled oath, concentrates the mind superbly. No police officer of any rank could allow himself to get into a situation that he could not control. He could not afford to. After all, there was only him. I once lay struggling with a prisoner in the middle of the street for thirty-five minutes while waiting for help to arrive in the early hours of a foggy November morning. It was complete stalemate; he was as knackered as I was. We just lay there in each other's arms like a pair of star-crossed lovers. We almost developed an affinity.

At the training school, of course, we had been taught a couple of golden rules in case we found ourselves in such a situation. First, we were instructed to 'flash our torch in the direction from where we thought help would come'! This completely overlooked the fact that ninety per cent of police torches would not light. That a hundred mazey alleys ran between the beleaguered copper and the rescuer was another important point that was overlooked.

The second hint was no more helpful than the first – 'Give three short, sharp blasts on your police-whistle.' Assuming the cut-throat opponent had permitted time to give this trio of signals, who was expected to hear it? Unless they were in the same alley, no one. And even if they were in the same alley and *did* hear the same whistle, would they have the faintest idea what it was? The only time that I have ever heard a police-whistle is in a radio play.

Because a man was vulnerable, he had to learn street-sense, and he had to learn it quick. He needed to know when to shout loud and when to talk quiet. Even the most innocuous of situations can become inflamed with the arrival of a flashing blue lamp and a dozen would-be rescuers.

This street-sense was typified by Charlie Rogers and his hot meat pie. Charlie had wandered off our manor in the early hours of the morning to purchase a hot pie at the all-night coffee stall at the nearby Elephant and Castle underground station. Being some half-mile off his beat, he made his way back by a sensible use of sidestreets. Quietly munching his pie, he turned a corner in time to stumble on an enormous gang-fight. Some forty men, armed with knives and razors, were laying about one another, each side giving as good as they received. Charlie, although not recognizing any of the participants, certainly recognized the types. Heroics aside, forty razor-slashing heavies are rather long odds for a lone copper, tooled up with a short wood truncheon and a hot meat pie.

In all the best television series, there would have been a convenient nearby call-box, or perhaps a zealous phone-owning tenant watching from an upstairs window. In reality, of course, the nearest call-box was half a mile away and vandalized beyond redemption. The phone-owning tenant had his head under the bed clothes and was 'not getting involved with that lot' for anyone. Now there are all sorts of suggestions as to what Charlie's best course of action should have been. This was, after all, a very serious matter – an affray, no less, for which seven-year sentences were almost commonplace. In addition, we cannot have gangs settling their differences on a public street, even if it is two in the morning.

Charlie, who had never harboured ambitions either to be the Commissioner or to receive the Queen's Police Medal for Gallantry, then did a very sensible thing. He sat down on a nearby wall and finished his pie. Eventually, when both gangs had withdrawn, taking their wounded with them, he too moved off and made his way back to the station.

When Charlie recounted the story to me some forty-five minutes later, I remember thinking what a good exam question it would make: 'You turn a corner in the early hours of the morning eating a hot meat pie. There you come face to face with forty well-armed men, all intent on killing each other. You are completely isolated and, except for your truncheon and your pie, totally unarmed. Describe your actions and give your reasons for them.' Much better, I thought, than all those boring acts and sections they usually ask about.

Later, four of us accompanied Charlie to the scene in a police van. The only visible signs of any previous activity were bloodstains in the road and a pie-wrapper behind a wall. No one had complained; no one had reported anything unusual; and Charlie appeared to be suffering from amnesia. It must have been pretty bad, too, because he bought another pie, obviously forgetting he had just eaten one.

Had there been any chance, however remote, that I might be tempted to sneer at Charlie for his inaction, it was dispelled some few weeks later. Together with Jimmy Davenport, I was leaving the station soon after eleven o'clock one mild spring night. Just as we were going down the station steps, Sergeant Billy Budd thrust his head out of the front office window.

'Have a look at the pub in Cobourg Road, Ginger. Woman's on the phone, reckons she can't sleep 'cause there's a disturbance outside.'

I pulled a bit of a face. 'It's the far end of the ground to my beat, sarge. It'll take me a good half an hour to walk there.'

'Good lad, it'll probably be all over by then.'

'What is it?'

'Nothing too serious, it's a skiffle group from the Beehive pub. She reckons they're practising outside.'

The manor had in fact become quite musical. Russ Conway, the leading pianist of the day, had just graduated from playing in a local pub. Tommy Steele was following Max Bygraves into doing something even more successful. Ruby Murray, a singer of acquired taste, lived a few streets from the station and found herself with no less than five records in the hit parade at the same time. The world of show business was also being strengthened by the talents of Michael Caine from the Old Kent Road and Charlie Drake from the Walworth Road. Rock stars and small-time celebrities were breaking out over the manor like pimples.

Jimmy decided to accompany me to the complaint. Ordinarily he would not have been quite so casual about this doubling-up. However, he had recently submitted his resignation and rightly guessed that no one would be exerting too much authority over him for his last few days in the force.

The Beehive in Cobourg Road was a small, family public house a short distance from the junction of Neate Street. We were about to turn the corner when Jimmy seized my arm.

'Listen!' he commanded.

I stopped and tilted my head.

'Can't you hear it? It's good!'

I could hear it right enough. It was a skiffle group and they were playing 'It takes a worried man to sing a worried song'. Jimmy was right, they were good. I glanced at my watch. It was just sixteen minutes to midnight. Okay, so they were a talented group, but for anyone trying to get to sleep even the Royal Philharmonic can be infuriating.

'Come on, Jim, we'll have to move them.'

'No, wait.' He nodded his head in time to the music and then began to sing, quite softly at first, then slowly increasing in volume, '. . . I'm worried now but I won't be worried long . . .'

I suddenly realized that Jimmy also was really quite

good. I sat down on a wall outside the park-keeper's house and just listened. Gradually the group went through a small repertoire and Jim seemed to know every word of every song. We had 'Grand Coolie Dam', 'Rambling Man' and 'Cumberland Gap' before a whole new sound cut rudely across the mild night air.

'Will you bleedin' pack it in? I've rung the law about you three times now and they're on their way 'ere. Let's get a bit of sleep for Gawd's sake!'

I sat up with a start. 'Rung the law three times'? That meant that someone else from the station must be on their way. I climbed quickly to my feet and brushed the brickdust from my trousers.

'Come on, Jim!' I said, cutting into the last line of 'Frankie and Johnnie'. 'You may be leaving the bloody job but I'm not!'

We walked the few yards to the street corner and there was the group still strumming merrily away, oblivious to all.

'Abaht time too!' called the harsh female voice. 'They've been 'ere a bloody hour already!'

Slipping into my official constabulary demeanour, I gave the group a few Now-come-along's and they went away happy enough. In fact I had barely ushered them away before Billy Budd appeared in the station Wolseley.

'Where've you two buggers been? I sent you up here an hour ago!'

'It is a long walk, sarge,' I complained. 'We got here just as fast as we could.'

Bill did not believe us, of course, but he was never one to make too much fuss, and besides, the call had been dealt with.

'Well, you've got an equally long walk back to your own beats. Incidentally, I don't expect you to take anywhere near as long to return. I'll see you both at the top of Walworth Road in . . .' he looked at his watch . . . 'half an hour, no, twenty minutes.' He gave a nod of satisfaction, slipped the car into gear and was gone.

'I really enjoyed that,' said Jim. 'The singing, I mean. It made a nice change.'

'Going to withdraw your resignation, then?'

'No chance! How about you? Are you going to stay here and plod around the beat for the next thirty years or are you going to show a bit of initiative?'

I was stung by this remark and angrily retorted, 'I'm putting in for the traffic patrol tomorrow, if you must know.'

'That's better,' agreed Jim, gazing disdainfully all around. 'It'll get you away from this hole anyway.'

Up until that moment I had not had the slightest intention of applying for traffic patrol. Now it seemed I had presented myself with a fait-accompli.

7. A lack of respect

Usually a night-duty copper would not stagger back to the station until a minute or so before booking-off time at 6 a.m. Sergeant Deal, the station officer, was therefore quite surprised when I wandered in soon after five o'clock.

'I want to apply for traffic patrol, sarge. What forms do I need?'

'Well, you could try a certificate of sanity,' he sniffed, as he looked up from his typing. 'Why on earth do you want to join "traf-pol"?'

'Well, I'm not sure I do, really, but I've got four years' service in now and I feel that I ought to have a go at something else.'

'I can never understand why any fool wants to ride motorbikes in ice and snow. You'll kill your bloody self.'

'One or two do survive, you know,' I pointed out.

'Yes, but you won't be one of them! Look at the state of you now. You've got an hour to go before you finish a night-duty and it's all you can do to stay awake!'

'Sergeant!' I spoke with slow deliberation. 'It's mainly because I get into this state on night-duty that I *am* applying for traffic patrol. I assume it hasn't escaped your attention that traf-pol do little or no night-duty?'

'True,' he agreed.

'Very well, that's why I would like to be one of them. That plus the fact that I rather fancy myself bombing down the by-pass at ninety.'

'Well, you'd better not give that as your reason for wanting to join.'

'Why not? That's why most blokes apply, isn't it?'

'Oh yes, I know it, you know it and "they" know it. The only difference is, that they don't *want* to know it. They want you to say that it has always been your lifelong ambition to facilitate London's traffic from the padded seat of a 500 twin Triumph. But I don't even know why we are discussing this, you've got no chance. How many traffic summonses did you do last month?'

'Er – traffic summonses, sarge?'

'Yes, "*traffic* summonses, sarge". I bet it wasn't half a dozen.'

I made no reply.

'Well, am I right?'

'I – er – I never count the amount of summonses I do. After all, they're not scalps to be hung on your belt, you know,' I reproved.

'Don't give me that crap! If you want traffic patrol, mate, you'd better start thinking about twenty summonses a week!'

'A week!'

'If, heaven forbid, you ever get as far as a selection board, that'll be what every other tear-arsed applicant who is competing against you will be clocking. Now how d'you feel?'

I shrugged as if this bombshell made no difference at all to me.

'I tell you this,' he went on, 'you've got no chance. Sam Parry would have to approve it, the Commander would have to approve it, then, if you were extremely lucky, you may get as far as a board.' His eyes narrowed thoughtfully. 'There is something I will do for you, though.'

I brightened up a little at this. It appeared that, if nothing else, I was about to receive a little advice or maybe even help.

'Yes, sarge?'

'I'll bet you a quid that you never get through the bloody board!'

'You're on.'

'Very well. You want form 728 and it has to be typed!' He shook his head in apparent wonder. 'You're not only wasting your time but it's going to cost you money as well! What a burk! On second thoughts perhaps you *should* go into traf-pol.' With that he left the office to bail a late prisoner.

I collapsed into bed about seven o'clock that morning and fell asleep instantly. Soon after eleven, though, I was wide awake with fantasies of sitting astride a roaring great Triumph. It had crossed my mind that I knew next to nothing about the function of traffic patrol. Some embittered coppers used to claim that the very title was a complete misnomer. 'They don't "do" any traffic and they never patrol,' I heard one once moan. Nowadays, the traf-pol is a highly specialized body, responsible for most of the capital's traffic arrangements – sudden diversions, accidents, vehicle removals and escorts, they undertake them all. In addition, each officer has an outstanding knowledge of traffic legislation *and* keeps that knowledge up to date. So except in emergencies, traffic patrol officers do not get caught up in the day-to-day routine of street policing: a street-duty copper will take on the task, thereby releasing the specialized officer for the job he has been trained for. The two departments are quite separate, and perhaps the average street copper does not always appreciate his colleagues' expertise. I know that until I applied for traffic patrol I certainly fell into this category. I was soon put right, however.

My application had been in some two weeks and I had already passed the first hurdle. This should have been my interview with Sam Parry. Sergeant Deal refused to believe that when I had submitted my application I had been unaware that it was the first day of Sam's annual leave. As a result, the interview was undertaken by his brand-new deputy, a freshly appointed chief inspector named Rupert Hill. Rupert knew as much about me as I knew about him and therefore could only base his recommendations on the strength of our interview. The result was I passed. First blood to me. Sadly it was too much to hope that everyone would be on annual leave right up until the final selection. All I could do, therefore, was wait and try to glean as much knowledge of traf-pol procedures as possible in the time that was left to me.

It was by now very late spring and an unusually cold early-turn had found me on a rush-hour traffic point. As usual, I had cut my arrival at the station very fine and had omitted to wear enough clothing to keep out the cold. By nine-thirty, when the traffic volume should have been waning, it was piling up even more heavily. In addition, I was cold and very hungry.

'There's been an accident down there, guv'nor!' called out a passing bus driver, nodding back over his shoulder.

'Sod!' Why is it people can't have accidents when I begin a traffic point and not when I am about to go for breakfast? I waved a reluctant acknowledgement and set off to find the trouble.

The cause of the accident and also of the traffic snarl-up was an old Bedford van. It had emerged slowly out of a side turning after its brakes had failed. To compound the misfortune, of the hundreds of cars streaming by, it managed to collide with the only Rolls-Royce of the morning. Fortunately no one was injured, but the rear nearside wing of the Rolls was badly buckled. The van had so many battle-scars scattered over its rusting body that one more did not show. I thought the owner of the Rolls was surprisingly good about the whole thing. He was far more tolerant than I would have been in such circumstances. He simply required an exchange of particulars and was prepared to leave it at that. The van driver, on the other hand, a certain Mr Charlie Jerroll, was something really special. If ever I was to compile a list of all-time cretins, he would be firmly in number one spot. He kept on and one about how the police always picked on him when he was on his way to an appointment. 'You do it on purpose, you know. You're all power-mad. I'm sure of it.'

I studied the van. Even *with* brakes it would have been a heap. The tread on the tyres and the road-tax were as inconspicuous as the brake-linings.

'Right, give him your name, address and insurance particulars,' I instructed. 'Then perhaps we can do something about your appointment. Where is it?'

'It's with the bank manager about halfway down the Walworth Road. I'm already late, so I don't want to get held up by the likes of you.'

'That's okay, mate, I see no problem,' I assured him. 'We'll just push your van into the side of the road and you can toddle off for your appointment. While you're gone I'll finish taking measurements and such like. Fair enough?'

'I s'pose so, although I can't see why I can't take the van with me. I mean how do I know you will be finished when I get back? I don't want to be sodded about all day. Some of us have work to do.'

'Listen,' I insisted through gritted teeth, 'while you are standing here rabbiting to me, you could be at the bloody bank. Now just leave me your ignition key and hop it!'

'Typical,' he snarled as he thrust the key into my palm and turned angrily in the direction of the bank. Meanwhile, the rather tolerant Rolls-Royce-owner, having obtained the necessary details, also moved away.

As soon as I was on my own, I hastened to a nearby sweetshop where I asked to use the telephone. I then dialled the emergency service and requested the attendance of traffic patrol for a vehicle inspection. Twenty minutes or so later, a huge old Humber estate car purred in behind the van and two overweight, middle-aged coppers emerged.

'Morning, shag. What can we do for you?' For some reason that I never did discover, all traffic patrols at the time had a habit of calling everybody else 'shag'.

I explained what had happened and asked them if they

could give me a list of as many offences as they could find on the van.

'Will do, shag,' said the taller one as he looked at the van disdainfully. 'What is it, a crop-sprayer?'

Within a few minutes they were underneath it, inside it and on top of it. They then went into a brief huddle with a clipboard. After a short conversation, the taller one spoke to me again.

'Well, shag, we've got seventeen offences for your mate. About the best thing to do with that –' he nodded to the van – 'is to push it off a long pier. Anything else we can do for you?' he added, handing me a sheet of paper.

'No, you've done wonders as it is. Thank you very much.'

'Any time, shag. Just call. Tat-ta.'

'Tat-ta,' I responded, already studying the list. There were offences on it I never knew existed. I began to look anxiously up and down the road for Mr Jerroll's return. I had a nagging feeling that not only was I about to be vindictive, but that I was also going to enjoy it.

Almost an hour after his departure, the driver returned to the scene. 'I hope you've finished because I've got a lot to do. Have you got my keys?'

'Yes, I've got your keys, Mr Jerroll, and I've also got something else.'

'Christ, what now? How long is this going to take?'

'Not two minutes, Mr Jerroll, then you can be on your way. Now I would like you to listen carefully. I have to point out the following offences. One . . .'

When I reached the tenth offence, I could not resist glancing up. Mr Jerroll did not look well. As I reached the last of the offences, I pointed out that the vehicle was also too dangerous to drive. I was by no means sure that I had the power to do this, on the other hand I had the key so there was not much he could do about it. All that concerned me was that I was already an hour and a half late for breakfast and there was no possible way I was going to chance him clouting something else in my vicinity.

Although I had been very impressed with the knowledge of the two traf-pol officers, in reality it had been disastrous for my confidence. Nuts and bolts mean nothing to me and I knew they never would. Just suppose I was to pass the board and one day some green copper was to ask me for a vehicle inspection? He would be lucky if I could even give him the tyre pressure.

Three weeks later I was ordered to attend an interview with the Commander. This was to be the second hurdle in my quest. It was apparent that the luck that had been with me on my first interview had deserted me badly on my second. Andrew Way had been promoted and a new man was installed. 'Dim-Tim' Tompkins was the absolute epitome of all Trenchard-Boys. As a Commander, I placed him a million light years away from me. In addition, he was arguably the worst speaker I have ever heard. Each sentence he uttered would be punctuated by at least two 'er's' and one 'um'. He was vague, indecisive and uninspiring.

I was ushered into his presence and waited for a seeming eternity while he perused my application. Finally there was some movement.

'Er – yes, um-er, Cole, isn't it?'

I agreed it was indeed Cole.

'Er – you want to join the, er, traffic patrol. Um, is that right?'

'That's quite right, sir.'

'I see.' He then gave two more 'um's' and for a moment appeared to be about to say something. Unfortunately the telephone then rang. This appeared to confuse him. 'Er – will you – er, wait outside while I answer the, um, phone?'

I slipped outside into the corridor, during which time he poured ten minutes of indecision into the handset. Finally I heard the receiver replaced. There was another ten-minute delay before he called me once more into the office.

'Er – let me see now, where, um, were we?'

77

'I've applied for traffic patrol, sir,' I reminded him.

'Ah! Oh yes, so you, er, have.'

Once more the telephone rang. I was already halfway towards the door before he again requested my absence. This time I waited outside even longer. The telephone had been replaced some fifteen minutes before I was recalled.

'Yes, er – Cole, yes. Now where were we? Um, I should think that'll be all right, er – wouldn't you?'

'Yes, sir,' I agreed, having not the faintest idea what he was talking about.

'Okay, I've, er, approved your, um, application. You will receive your final selection, er, board in, um, about a week or two. Thank you.'

'How did you possibly get through this time?' asked Sergeant Deal incredulously.

'I simply assisted the Commander with a couple of phone calls, sergeant. He appears to have difficulty with these modern inventions.'

'Well, that'll be an asset on a motorbike, I must say.' He shook his head in disgust. 'When's your final board selection?'

'In a couple of weeks.'

At that reply Deal laughed uproariously. 'You'll be night-duty again by that time. You know what you're like night-duty. It'll be like interviewing a dormouse! You wait, mate, you won't be able to fluke it this time. They'll have your guts for garters,' he added prophetically.

I was required to report for my interview at Balham Police Station, which was a convenient twenty-five-minute cycle ride from home. This location was the only good news; everything else about it was disastrous. To begin with, it was on the afternoon after my first night-duty stint of the month. This was always a bad period for me. I would feel totally 'punchy', my metabolism still not adjusted to the drastic change of hours. Secondly, it was scheduled for 2 p.m. This would mean that after washing, shaving and a midday breakfast, I would have had a maximum of four hours' sleep. Finally, we were to attend in full uniform, minus helmet. This would entail transporting all my equipment on the handlebars of my cycle. I just hoped it was a dry day.

It wasn't that I failed to set the alarm, it was simply that I slept right through it. The storm finally awoke me a little after three o'clock. Panic-stricken, I hurtled around the flat. I knew that whatever else, I must shave. Bundling my uniform jacket into a bag, I downed a quick glass of milk and leapt on to my bicycle.

The rain was falling in stair-rods and slanting into my face. Although Balham was barely five miles away, it was uphill all the way. Pedalling furiously and weaving in and out of the traffic, I reached there in just over twenty minutes. My clothes and body were saturated both with perspiration and with rain. It was also half past three.

Swinging into the station yard, I saw a handwritten notice that read 'Traf-pol interviews first floor'. I dumped my cycle and raced up the stairs. There I was greeted by a grey-haired sergeant with a clipboard.

'Who the bleedin' hell are you?'

I fought for breath for a moment or two before panting, '604 Cole, sarge. I'm here for an interview.'

'You mean you were *supposed* to be here for an interview,' he glanced at his watch, 'an hour and a half ago to be precise. And just look at the state of you! Where have you come from, the Isle of Man?'

'I overslept, sarge.'

'Go on, you didn't, did you? Well, I tell you what, I'da never believed it if you hadn't told me. I would just've thought you always went around like that.' He shook his head a few times before adding, 'What exactly are you, a diver or something?'

He stared for a while in silent disbelief. Finally, after studying both me and his clipboard for some time, he spoke again.

'Look, son,' he said kindly, 'I'll slot you in at the end.

It's just possible you may get away with it. I'll announce you as if that was your place in the queue all the time. In the meantime I suggest you get yourself into the senior officers' washroom and straighten your bloody self up.'

'Thanks, sarge. Thanks a lot!'

He pointed down the corridor with his pen. 'It's the second on the left. You should be okay. The only senior ranks here today are in there on the interviewing board. I would reckon you've got about twenty-five minutes, although by the state of you an hour wouldn't be enough.'

I thanked him yet again and squelched down the corridor and into the washroom. I was fully aware that I was not cutting a dashing figure, but I was not prepared for just how scruffy I was. I was practically steaming! As I looked in the mirror I saw that a dark wet ring encircled the entire collar of my shirt, my hair was matted and sweat ran unabated down my face. In addition, my boots and trouser bottoms were splattered with street mud.

Twenty minutes, he had said. Very well, I thought, I'll strip down and have a warm water wash. I hung my clothes and the bag over a lukewarm radiator and began furiously to splash water over myself. I had just slipped into the swing of it, with waves slurping across the chill tiled floor, when the door swung open.

It was difficult to say who was the more surprised. The sergeant had told me I was safe for twenty minutes but had obviously forgotten that even senior officers need to respond to a call of nature and a cigarette. On the other hand, any superintendent slipping out for a quick fag does not expect to see a totally naked stranger hurling water everywhere in the gents.

At this stage, I should explain the procedural requirements of a constable who meets any officer of senior rank. He acknowledges the senior presence by the expression 'All correct'. This is of course irrespective of whether it *is* all correct or not. In reality, all hell could be loose; it is simply an inbuilt practice of the force. I had my mouth open to make this statutory greeting, when I closed it again. I felt stupid enough as it was.

As a result of this change of mind on my part, we never spoke at all. In fact we totally ignored each other. He stood facing the urinal wall puffing furiously on his unlit cigarette while I did my best to dry my most intimate parts on a ridiculously high roller-towel.

Just as soon as the door closed behind him, I raced to the radiator and began to dress. Sizeable sections of me were still wringing wet but my clothes were so damp it barely mattered. I reached into the bag and slid out my uniform jacket, dropping it in instant dismay. I had brought the wrong one! My armlet, whistle-chain and numerals were all secreted safely on my other jacket hanging quietly in my bedroom cupboard.

There was only one thing for it, I simply had to brazen it out. Smoothing down the garment, I walked calmly out of the gents and into the presence of the clipboard sergeant.

'What the –!' he began. 'Where's the rest of your uniform?'

'In a cupboard at home, sarge.'

'Oh, that's magic! That's absolutely bloody marvellous! You arrive an hour and a half late, you look like a tramp and you haven't got a soddin' uniform! They're goin' to fall over themselves to accept you for traffic patrol, they are! 'Ere, you're not barmy, are you?'

'Well, there's nothing I can do about it now, sarge,' I replied, ignoring the question of my sanity. 'I'll just have to front it out.'

Just then the door from the interview room opened and a white-faced young constable emerged.

'They said give 'em five minutes, sarge, then send in the last man.'

Before he closed the door behind him I glimpsed three humourless-looking men seated behind a large desk. The middle one was my companion from the gentlemen's toilet.

'Right,' said the sergeant, addressing himself once more to me. 'I take it you've got your pocket book? They will want to see what sort of work you've been doing lately.'

I said nothing but ever so slightly shook my head.

'It's-in-your-jacket-at-home-in-your-cupboard?' He nodded his head in time to each word. 'Silly me, fancy not realizing that.' He closed his eyes and tilted back his head in an air of mock despair.

After a couple of minutes of total silence, the sergeant beckoned me with his board. 'Right, in you go. I wouldn't bother to shut the door if I was you, you won't be in there long enough.'

He ushered me in with all due reverence.

'Close the door, will you, sergeant,' came the command from the table.

'Sir!' acknowledged the sergeant as he clicked it shut. I resisted a smirk with great difficulty.

The interviewing trio consisted of the superintendent whose acquaintance I had already made, plus two chief inspectors.

'Name?' asked the superintendent without looking up.

'Cole, sir.'

He made a quick note then lifted his head. He stared in amazement for a few seconds but said nothing.

The chief inspector on his left held up a form 728 with just a few lines of writing upon it. 'Yours?' he asked.

I bent forward and instantly recognized my writing. 'Yes.'

'Not much, is it? You haven't told us a thing about yourself. Age, service and the distance you live from the nearest garage. Other than that you said nothing.'

'Well, I thought you would consider any more than that to be bullshit.'

'Of course it would be bullshit! That's what we are here for! All interviews are bullshit!' He lifted up several well-filled 728s. 'Look, these are the applications of your competitors. Every one of them bullshit! Some of them have written up to two and three pages. You did eight lines.'

'What is the current road safety campaign in your area?' asked the second chief inspector.

'Road safety campaign?'

'Yes, road safety campaign. You do know we run them, I suppose?'

'Oh, er, Mind-that-child?'

'That was *last* year. Is there any chance of you being just a little more topical?'

While I struggled for an answer, the first chief inspector cut in. 'You are stationed, I believe, at Carter Street?'

'Yes.'

'Very well, who garages his car there?'

I knew I looked blank.

'Come, come. The chauffeur of a very senior officer at Scotland Yard lives on your manor. Each night he leaves the car in your station yard. Whose car is it?'

I suddenly remembered seeing a big black Humber motor car parked from time to time next to our stables. Although I had not the faintest idea whose car it was, I suddenly thought of something that should have impressed them no end.

'Oh, you mean KYU 604,' I answered matter-of-factly.

The reason for this startling knowledge of police registration numbers was solely because it coincided with my own divisional number – 604.

'Well, if you know the number of the car, you must know whose it is, then,' he responded illogically.

'I'll make it easier for you and give you a clue,' announced the second chief inspector.

No, please don't do that, I thought. I knew I would never guess the name in a month of Sundays. If he was to make it easier and I still did not know it, I would seem an even bigger idiot.

'He's the Assistant Commissioner.'

Disaster was imminent. The fact that I did not know who left a confounded car in our yard would pale into insignificance beside not knowing the name of the Assistant Commissioner. For the purpose of interviews, at least, chief inspectors believe that PCs should recite the names of each senior officer in the force three times nightly before going to sleep. I was done and I knew it.

The superintendent opened up for the first time. 'I would have been more impressed with your knowledge of the AC's registration number if it had not coincided with your own divisional number.' He had obviously just read the three figures from my brief application.

To confirm this number theory, all three sets of eyes lifted to my epaulettes, my *empty* epaulettes. I closed my eyes and waited for the next few words. Almost in unison they came: 'Where are your numerals? Your armlet? Your whistle and your chain?'

'I'm afraid they are at home in my bedroom. I overslept and forgot them.' I shrugged helplessly, all that I wanted to do was to get out of that building as quickly as possible.

'Is that why you were prancing around in the nude and chucking water everywhere?' asked the superintendent.

I nodded. The two chief inspectors looked quickly at the questioner as if the pair of us had shared some unmentionably erotic experience.

'Well, for what it's worth,' he went on, 'before you leave this interview – never to return, I might add – I would like to point out something very important to you. You have been in here for some ten minutes and you have managed to say the word "sir" just once. Well, once is not enough. When you are wondering why you failed this interview, forget about oversleeping, forget about the wrong jacket, in fact forget about forgetting. Just remember respect. That is why you failed, young man, and that alone.'

Six hours later I walked into the front office at Carter

Street having given KYU 604 just a cursory glance. I held out a crumpled pound note to the station officer.

'If I pay you the bet straight away, sarge, instead of waiting for payday, will you promise to ask no questions?'

'My lips are sealed, son, my lips are sealed. You wouldn't have liked motorbikes anyway.'

8. Lucretia Borgia and others

My failure to be a traffic patrol officer had, at least for me, one serious side-effect. Every time there was a traffic problem on the manor I would be placed into the thick of it. By 'the thick of it' I mean slap-bang in the middle of the road. If water mains blew up, gas pipes exploded or traffic lights failed, the resultant chaos would always require the attention of at least one uniformed constable. Me.

'Let me see, now, who can we put on it? Ginger! You're a bit of a traffic expert, ain't you? Didn't you apply for the traf-pol or something a while back? You're just the bloke for this job. The council are digging up the road at . . .' At least once a week I would hear that sort of discussion.

The truth of the old saying, 'There's more out than in' is never better illustrated than half an hour spent on any traffic point. After such a spell, one realizes that even to cross a road can be as hazardous as a month up the Amazon. There is a mania that permeates the most innocent of people once they are behind the wheel of a car. Uncle Ted and Auntie Ada in that clapped-out jalopy will battle bus-drivers like kamikaze pilots, while stripe-shirted reps in Ford saloon cars will jockey Le Mans-like at traffic lights. Motorcyclists, meanwhile, will weave and change lanes as if they are impervious to substance. The frailer their machine, the more chances they will take. If this belligerence is bad, the persecution-complex is overwhelming. A young police constable soon realizes that no motorist in the history of the internal combustion engine has ever driven through anything other than a green traffic light at twenty-eight miles an hour, or parked more than two minutes on a double yellow line. I soon came to the conclusion that this must be true because every motorist I ever spoke to assured me it was.

'On my muvver's life I ain't bin more than one minute, guv'nor, honest. Ask the missus, she'll tell yer, won't yer, Lil?'

'That's right,' Lil would say, 'although to be really honest, Sid, I thought it was more like half a minute.'

The fact that the entire nearside lane had been totally paralysed for the last three-quarters of an hour, would have completely escaped both Sid and Lil's attention.

There was one road-user on the manor, however, who had more sheer brazen nerve than a platoon of medal winners. He should by rights have been squashed hideously at least a dozen times daily. Bert Coppins was a dedicated roadsweeper. His kerbs and gutters almost sparkled. Nothing was permitted to stand between Bert-the-brush and a clean drainhole, least of all a seventy-five-seater, double-decker, bright red London Transport omnibus.

The main traffic point on our manor was at the junction of Camberwell New Road and Brixton Road. This junction took an enormous volume of vehicles. To make matters worse, on the bend, just a few yards from the traffic lights, three busy lanes converged into two. Buckled bumpers and grazed wings abounded daily as great diesel lorries and small family bangers dangerously intermingled. In and out of the hooting, exhaust-laden air, Bert would bounce the broom with a dexterity that was a pleasure to behold. Eight bus routes squeezed through that bottleneck and each of them seemed determined to kill him.

'Bert!' I would exclaim almost daily. 'Will you get out of the bloody road? You'll get yourself killed here one day!'

'Don't you worry, Ginger me-lad, I'm all right. The buses won't 'urt yer. It's the bleedin' cyclists you 'ave ter watch out for!'

He would then go into his daily story of how he was knocked down by one while sweeping Westminster Bridge.

It didn't matter how many times Bert told me the story, I always listened to it as if I was hearing it afresh. The reason for this tolerance was twofold. First, I was convinced he was living on borrowed time and wished to extend to him every courtesy. The second was it made me laugh.

He had, it seemed, been offered some Sunday overtime in order to sweep part of Westminster Bridge, either before or after some ceremonial function. It was decided to carry out this operation at seven o'clock in the morning when the bridge would be deserted. Now, in comparison with most other London bridges, Westminster is particularly wide and at 7 a.m. on a Sunday it would look as empty and broad as a Himalayan plateau. Having the bridge to himself, Bert whistled cheerfully in the early morning sunshine. Unfortunately, the bridge was no longer his sole prerogative. Another user was approaching fast from the south side. A leather-shorted, drop-handlebarred, cycle-capped racer was out for an early morning training spin.

It may well be that the bright early sunshine of a pleasant spring Sunday does lull people into a false sense of security. Whatever the reason, there were just two people at that location and neither of them was aware of the other. That is, they were not aware until the front wheel of the cycle struck the backside of the sweeper. It was questionable whether the cyclist had even lifted his head until both Bert and his broom had left the ground. The pain of Bert's broken collar bone was only matched by that of the cyclist's shattered wrists.

'Just me on the bleedin' bridge in bright sunshine at seven in the morning and the silly barstard still knocks me down! I tell yer, Ginger, they're a bloody menace, them bikes.'

I could only marvel at the unpredictability of fate. Smacked to the ground on a desolate bridge, yet daily surviving the furious hordes of London rush-hour traffic. Sooner or later, I knew, he would be just jam on the road, but until that happened I revelled in his survival.

It was around the mid-fifties that the Metropolitan Police slowly became aware that it had a traffic problem. We – that is, the police – knew that thousands of people drove into the Metropolis in the morning and out again in the evening. Other than assisting them in this toing and froing, we did little else. Many times towards the end of their traffic points I heard PCs exclaim, 'Where on earth do they all go to?' Where indeed. Every main, secondary and minor road within a ten-mile radius of Piccadilly seemed to be used as a rat-run to the centre of town. Along each of them an almost unbroken line of traffic would flow. What happened when they reached there, wherever 'there' was? In effect they simply parked anywhere. Double yellow lines, factory entrances, private forecourts (other people's, of course) and, very often, just in the centre of the road. A few uniformed constables would be instructed to summon the most blatant offenders but by and large it was like baling out the sea.

The attitude of offenders who were booked was nearly always belligerent. 'How about all those other cars?' was a stock answer. To be a driver of a badly parked car in a street of badly parked cars certainly fostered a sense of security. This attitude slowly began to change with the formation of the traffic removal squad (TRS). This small band of traffic patrol officers simply descended on a badly obstructed street and removed every vehicle in it. It mattered not that the car had been there three hours or three minutes. The TRS had no favourites, they hated everyone. If it was there, then it went.

This was all very well in theory but when twenty vehicles had been moved from a street, what then? I mean, where does one put them? Certainly not in police station yards, most of which are too small for hopscotch. This problem was finally resolved by using temporary sites – areas where demolition had taken place but no rebuilding was immediately planned. The first of these car-pounds was a huge expanse at the south-west foot of Vauxhall Bridge. It was there that the removal squad began to bring the offending vehicles.

Although traffic patrol drivers ferried these cars to the site, they wanted no part in restoring them to their owners. There was one simple reason for this – aggravation. Private motorists were simply not used to being inconvenienced and if they were, then someone was going to get a right earful. This 'someone' was never the person who removed the vehicle, it was always the poor chump who restored it. Nowadays drivers are more battle-conditioned; they tend to be quite philosophical. In comparison to those early times, life in the car-pound now is almost tranquil. Yet today, not only has the driver temporarily lost ownership of his car, but he has to pay an exorbitant fee to recover it. Then, he paid nothing. The sheer inconvenience was considered punishment enough.

If the elite of the traffic patrol was not prepared to restore the vehicles to the lawful owners, then who was? Well, of course, there was no real choice: when in doubt, use a couple of expendable coppers. I was seconded there for just two weeks and it cured me of traffic patrol forever. What an insight into human behaviour! Even little grey-haired octogenarians were aggressive. 'Why was my car removed – eh? Go on, tell me that,' was the first reaction. Unfortunately the person doing the restoring never knew the answer to this. Illegally parked yes, they had all been removed for that, but nothing more explicit would ever be shown in the 'Vehicles IN' book.

At least a dozen people every day claimed to be on intimate terms with the Commissioner. One week at a car-pound and one realizes that the Commissioner of Police must be the greatest socialite in creation. Not only were they his friends but they were all going to complain about me. Me? All I was doing was giving them their rotten car back. Never a word of complaint about the bandit who removed it in the first place. In any case, I could never understand people who claimed some sort of connection to very senior ranks. The average constable faced with this situation will *always* but always summons them *and* do so with the greatest of pleasure! It is like striking a blow for the working classes.

Those who were unfortunate enough not to know the Commissioner or even the Home Secretary probably had but ten days to live. It was either that, or they were on errands of great mercy. I had never before met such noble people as I did in that short spell at the pound. Aggressive they may have been – but God, they were noble. 'I suppose that this is all one can expect from the police for giving one's time so freely to society.' This statement would then be followed by a great resigned sigh and a despairing shake of the head. Everyone, it seemed, had a complaint. When I restored a Ford Popular to a rabbi, I thought at last I had a customer who might be a little forgiving. He waited until he was in possession of his car and the paperwork completed, then made an allegation of theft – five cigarettes and a Milky Way!

On the other hand, one did meet some genuinely unlucky drivers, the most unfortunate of these being a bill-poster. Unbeknown to him, he stopped his vehicle in a street which was in the process of being cleared. In fact the car immediately behind him already had a removal officer on board and was just about to drive away. He leaped out of his three-wheeled van and ran across the pavement to a hoarding and slapped on a four-by-two poster. As he had slipped out of the driving seat, so someone else had slipped in. Meanwhile, having stuck the poster into position, he stepped back momentarily to admire his work. Giving a nod of satisfaction, he turned just in time to see his van disappearing down the street, all of sixty seconds after he had parked it.

Some people, of course, had a genuine reason for complaint. None more so than the white-faced lorry driver who, after his lorry had bounced into the pound, was seen to slip down from the top of the load where he had been fastening the ropes.

There was at least one type, however, who would not be belligerent. In fact they were usually quite the reverse. Glancing at their watch every few seconds, they would slip furtively into the office and whisper their registration number across the counter. This was always done in such a quiet voice that one usually had to ask them at least once to repeat it. These would be the drivers of either sex who had been caught out in some liaison. To have their vehicle removed in such circumstances was embarrassing enough for the men, but for the women it felt calamitous, mainly because it was usually their husband's car! The Kingston housewife who was expected to have spent the morning in Sainsbury's can be hard put to explain to her spouse just why his car was removed from Pimlico. The giveaway was always the question, 'Will this be reported to my husband? You see – well, it's all a little embarrassing really – he doesn't *like* me driving his car when he's not supervising it. You understand, I'm sure.'

'Your secret's safe with me, love,' was an answer that was guaranteed to fetch the smile back to her face.

Although I enjoyed providing this reassurance to those in distress, I must confess to sharing in a cruel trick played on one unfortunate young lady. Her Morris saloon had been removed from a mews in South Kensington where it had been partially blocking the entrance. It was immediately obvious to all on her arrival that wherever she should have been that day, South Kensington was not that place. I checked the book and found that her car had been in our possession for more than three hours. By chance, the driver who had brought it in had just returned with another vehicle, this time an Allard sports car.

'It is all right, is it?' she asked anxiously. 'The car, I mean. You see, I shouldn't really have been there.'

The quick spin in the Allard had obviously placed my vehicle-removal friend in a carefree state of mind. He beckoned the lady to the office sidedoor which faced out over the pound. The whole site was situated alongside the river edge. The ground was studded with remnants of wide old walls and pitted with deep derelict cellars. Because of these hazards, a police driver collected the cars from the outermost corners of the pound and handed them over to their owners at the office door.

'Now, let me see,' he said thoughtfully. 'You are the lady who had the Morris, aren't you?'

'That's right. There's nothing wrong, is there? You see my husband . . .'

'Oh no! Nothing to worry about really. I should think that after a week or two you'd barely notice it.'

'A week or two! Whatever is wrong? What have you done to it, for God's sake?'

'Well, I had a slight accident. It wasn't my fault really. Ginger here was mainly to blame.'

I looked up in dismay. 'Me??' I mouthed silently.

'What is it, what have you done?' She turned and almost screamed at me.

'He didn't do it on purpose, you understand. It was a genuine mistake.' He turned to me. 'Wasn't it, Ginger?'

'Where is my husband's car?' she interrupted. 'Show it to me, I want to see what you maniacs have done to it.'

'Well, perhaps I'd better explain first, just in case it comes as too much of a shock when you see it.' He gave a deep sigh then continued, 'You see, when I fetched your car in, some three hours ago, I knew we were going to be busy, so in order to leave room, I decided to park it at the far end. That's the end nearest the river. Well, I asked Ginger here to see me back, so I could get as close to the river as possible!' He paused and shook his head.

'Go on,' she whispered, fatefully closing her eyes.

'Well, I'm afraid he wasn't really paying attention. The long and short of it is that your car fell in the river.'

'Oh my God!'

'We got it out fairly quick, though. What we've decided to do, is to put it up on one of those walls. It'll get quite a good breeze up there. I've left all the doors wide open so it should be dry in no time. It might take a week or two to get rid of the smell, though.'

She slumped down into a rickety cane-backed chair and dropped her head in her hands.

'Unless, of course – ' He cut short his words. 'Yours was the *blue* Morris, I suppose?'

She raised her eyes with just a faint glimmer of hope. 'No, no, mine is a black car.'

'Oh, a black one! Oh well, that's different, you should've said so! Your car is fine! It's parked just around the back.'

She stared at him for seemingly ages. 'I think I should kill you but I'm so relieved that . . .' She shook her head and left the sentence unfinished.

'Oh well, I'm off now, Ginger,' he announced, rubbing his hands enthusiastically. 'I'll see if I can find myself a Mercedes this time.'

'Are they all like him?' she asked as the door closed.

I nodded. 'Most of 'em are.'

She stood up and smoothed down her dress. 'In that case I will have to get even with that sod. I thought I would never be able to look my husband in the face again.'

She undid her handbag and produced her driving licence as proof of her identity. 'Do you need me to sign something or other?' she asked, pen poised.

'Yes.' I swung the book towards her and pointed to the next vacant line. 'Scrawl it here and you can go without a stain on your character.'

She scribbled a quick signature and almost ran to her unblemished car. As she roared out of the gate I turned the book around and glanced idly at the name. She had certainly had the last laugh. I would show it to her tormentor when he returned. Perhaps it may worry him just a little. Lucretia Borgia indeed!

9. Let 'im 'ave yer!

Around this period of my service a great scandal hit the division. It had been common practice for two uniformed men, usually a sergeant and a constable, to be posted out in plain clothes for a month to deal with the problem of street-bookmakers. Usually, although not always, this short assignment took place on a neighbouring manor where the two coppers were less likely to be identified. Just a handful of men from each station would take part in this exercise. Unfortunately it appeared that someone had been at the 'take', although there was no positive proof who the someone was, or even which station he came from. The customary police procedure in these cases is pure overkill. The sure way of punishing the offender is to transfer everyone on the division who has ever worked 'bookies'. The result is that for one unproven allegation, twenty men are transferred. Apart from the sheer injustice of this, a stigma will follow the innocent for years. Take casual canteen conversation, for example.

'I see we've got a new fellow learning beats. Bit old for a recruit, isn't he?'

'Yes, he was apparently transferred under a cloud, something to do with street-bookmakers.'

Now when twenty men are transferred in these circumstances, nineteen innocents will suffer too. Because of this action, the division not only lost twenty experienced policemen, but it required a further batch to replace them. Who better, then, to fill a gap than a failed traf-pol applicant?

To be out 'on bookies' had the great advantage that one

worked bookies' hours, usually midday until 2 p.m. with just an occasional evening for dog-racing. Because of the recent scandal, senior officers gave great play to briefing. Although this was understandable, it was not very helpful. To a man, senior officers knew next to nothing about street-bookmakers.

Each briefing stressed over and over again the need to avoid 'perchers', or 'stick-ups' as they were usually called. These terms related to the bookmaker's practice of paying someone else to be arrested. These actors would stand on a pitch, usually by appointment, until they were taken off to the station to be charged. There they would give a false name and address and be bailed. After a quick guilty plea next morning in court the bookmaker would pay the fine plus a couple of pounds to the stick-up. Everyone would then be happy until the next month when another pair of coppers appeared and the whole charade began again.

The problem with not accepting stick-ups was that it then became a vastly more difficult job. Disguises would be worn and elaborate plans made, but the street-bookmaker would in ninety-nine per cent of cases see straight through the disguises. In addition to that, his customers were always on the look-out for coppers preparing to pounce. The result of this dilemma was that each pair of officers listened attentively to the warning about stick-ups and then promptly went out and nicked one!

I did five spells on bookies within that year and nearly always worked a stick-up system. Each manor had on average some sixteen pitches, usually secreted away in some backstreet or alley, making any approach by a stranger very difficult indeed. To begin this approach, I borrowed my father's car and together with an old prewar sergeant made a round of each of the pitches. I parked the car some distance from the pitch yet in a position that could be clearly seen by the look-out. We then sat tight and waited.

Within a few minutes the owner of both the pitch and a

statutory camel-hair coat would arrive and ask us how long we were working the area. We would tell him and he would then ask what day we proposed to 'visit' him.

'What day would you like, mon?' Sergeant Griffiths would say.

Every bookie would state a preference for a weekday. The last two or three on our list of course had no choice, there would only be Saturdays remaining on our rota.

'Well, if it has to be a Saturday, guv'nor, come early. It's ever such a busy day.'

'Quarter past twelve suit you?' asked Taff.

'Can't you make it twelve?'

'Twelve it is, mon!'

The practice would then be for us to arrive punctually on the agreed date. After a short stroll down the alley the bookie would be seen standing at the far end gesturing towards an anonymous-looking youth, half-hidden in a doorway. This youth would have a pencil and book in his hand, together with a pocketful of loose change and a dozen betting slips.

'Okay, boyo,' Taff would say. 'You're off!'

'Boyo' and us would then walk to the nearest police station where he would be charged with gaming in the street.

'How about bail?' the station officer would ask. 'Has he got a permanent address?'

'Yes,' Griff would say. 'It's all been checked out, he'll be at court right enough tomorrow morning.' And of course he always was, he had to be because the bookie would never pay him until the case had been heard.

There would be one important thing to remember at this stage. It was vital that the name of the stick-up used was one that he could spell! One academic I once arrested claimed his name was Henry Forsythe. I happily accepted this and thought no more about it until the station officer asked him if it was Forsythe with or without an 'e'.

'I'm not sure,' answered the puzzled prisoner.

'Not sure!' echoed the station officer. 'Not sure of your own bloody name?' He slid a pen across the desk top and added, 'Show me how you would normally spell it, then.'

The prisoner took up the pen and with slow deliberation wrote 'Henree Forsifeg'.

'Were you gaming in the street?' the magistrate would ask next morning.

'I'm afraid I was, sir.'

'How much did he have on him, officer?'

'Nine pounds ten shillings, sir.'

'Very well, fined five pounds. Can you pay it now?' The prisoner would shoot a furtive glance to the back of the court where the camel-hair coat was standing. The coat would give the merest of nods.

'Yes, sir.'

'This way,' would call the gaoler. The bookie would join the prisoner at the cash desk, the payment made and justice done.

This rota system was not of course unique to bookies – prostitutes had always been arrested in that way. These ladies would ensure their arrest took place during their menstruation to avoid any loss of earnings. Bookmakers, on the other hand, did not have menstrual cycles (although if their case came up on a Saturday it would be easy to believe they had). The fine and the couple of quid for the prisoner never bothered them unduly, but to spend a morning at court would be infuriating. One way in which to speed up this process was to use only experienced 'stick-ups'. Unfortunately this was not always practical. 'Stick-ups' were usually out-of-work drifters or small-time unsuccessful crooks. By definition they were not the most reliable of characters. All sorts of disasters could befall them in even the simplest of cases.

One enterprising stick-up was arrested and bailed at 12.30 p.m. at Peckham by Jock Simpson, a footballing friend of mine. Forty-five minutes later, under a different name, he was again arrested and bailed, this time at

Clapham. While this unquestionably showed great initiative, it did present a problem for the following morning. Namely, how to appear at two courts, at the same time, five miles apart.

As if the situation was not interesting enough, he celebrated a prospective double pay-out just a little too much and was arrested that night for drunk and disorderly at Bow Street. The station officer at Bow Street did him one great favour – he refused him bail. This at least saved the prisoner from the dilemma of knowing which court to attend the following morning.

On that morning, the arresting officer and the bookmaker, neither of them aware of the stick-up's triple identity, impatiently paced the entrance hall to Lambeth Court.

'I'll kill him, I will, I'll kill him,' muttered the bookmaker as he studied his watch every fifteen seconds.

'Look,' announced Jock finally. 'I'll have to go in court and explain to the magistrate that the prisoner hasn't turned up.'

'How long you reckon we've got?' asked the bookmaker anxiously.

'Well, we're eighteenth on the list and number twelve is on already – say twenty minutes at the most.'

'I'll see what I can do.'

Jock shrugged impassively and walked into court. As the seventeeth case of the morning drew to a close, Jock moved towards the witness box to ask for an adjournment.

'Case number eighteen, Your Worship,' announced the gaoler. 'Thomas Wood.'

'Excuse me, Your Wor–' began Jock.

'This way, Mr Wood,' continued the gaoler.

Jock could hardly believe his eyes. Twenty-four-year-old, slightly built Thomas Wood had aged forty years and added four stone overnight! This Thomas Wood was sixty-five if he was a day *and* he had a wooden leg!

'Sorry I'm late,' wheezed the prisoner. 'Bit of chest

trouble, sir. Always the same when I'm nervous.'

The magistrate, who was no stranger to respiratory ailments himself, gave a sympathetic nod.

If chest discomforts could really be brought about by nerves, then Jock Simpson should never have drawn another breath. We'll never get away with this, he thought. What kind of street-bookmaker has bronchitis and a wooden leg? The first Thomas Wood had been born in 1933, this one must have been at least seven at the turn of the century! If that magistrate had read the date of birth on the charge-sheet, then Jock was a stone-bonker certainty for six months for conspiracy! The formalities of the case were over in a couple of minutes, although to Jock it was an eternity. Thomas Wood was fined five pounds and given a word of advice from His Worship.

'I am sure you agree, Mr Wood, that a gentleman of your years should be looking for something a little less arduous than street-bookmaking? To be frank, I think you are a little past it. I would not therefore expect to see you before me again.'

'No, sir, you're right, sir. I think I'll give it a miss from now on.'

'Good man,' concluded His Worship.

Of course, not all bookmakers were fortunate enough to have their chesty old father-in-laws to hand. Yet it is interesting to note that a 'Thomas Wood' also arrived at the same time that morning at South-Western Court, where a bum-pouting constable must have been equally perturbed.

Many street-bookmakers lived on their nerve-ends. A new face in the street, roadworks, or a different milkman, could easily be a determined copper with aspirations of a 'good knock-off'. The attraction of arresting the bookie, or principal as he would be referred to at court, was that he was obviously the big fish. Fines in such cases could be as high as £50; small wonder, therefore, that stick-ups were so popular.

It was during my very first week on street-bookies that

this nervousness was to provide some embarrassment. My mother-in-law was extremely keen on a flutter and regularly trotted down to the local pitch at Chrysell Road to put on her two-bob each-way bet. Now such was the revenue in these small bets that once a year the bookmaker would hire a coach and take all his lady punters to the seaside for the day. Being one of his regular customers, she would carry the occasional bet from neighbours and workmates. On the big race days, therefore, she would find herself placing bets for as many as twenty or thirty people. In such circumstances one has to be particularly careful that everything is written down correctly. Punters do tend to become a little touchy if their thirty-to-one longshot romps home and only they know about it. Suitably armed with a long list and margin notes, she approached the pitch on Grand National day.

'Now look here, Ernie,' she began. 'There's one or two things I'd better explain first.' With that she spent the next few minutes detailing the complicated wishes of hopeful punters. Subsequently reaching the end of the list, she waited for Ernie's comments and queries. Receiving none – and that was not at all like Ernie – she raised her head from the list. Not only was Ernie no longer in sight but in his place stood a uniformed police inspector. Realizing that both my in-laws would visit the Chrysell Road pitch on National day, Taff and I had deliberately avoided it. Unknown to us, the early-turn duty officer had unfortunately decided to pay it a visit.

'Yes, madam, you were saying?' he asked.

Madam may well have *been* saying but madam was to say no more. She froze open-mouthed, with her queries, her selections and her stakes.

'You don't happen to be the bookmaker by any chance, do you?' he persisted.

She shook her head violently.

'Only it's just that you seem to have such a considerable number of racing selections.' He took the list from her and studied it momentarily. 'Oh well,' he continued as he handed it back, 'the pitch does not appear to be operating today. Pity, I felt lucky. I suppose we may as well go home?' She nodded rapidly in silent agreement as he walked to his car.

The Chrysell Road pitch was not only the nearest to my in-laws' home but also the nearest to mine. It was because of this geographical factor that a year later Taff and I arranged a rare Saturday stick-up there. I was going to a wedding that day and needed to leave work as soon as possible. The arrangements were that Taff and I were to call at the pitch soon after midday. Once the stick-up had been 'arrested', both he and Taff would make their way back to the station and I would go home in order to collect Joan and prepare for the wedding.

As we turned into the street, Ernie was standing in the doorway of the saloon bar of the King's Head. He gave the customary nod towards a spotty-faced youth who was busily engaged in taking bets halfway down the street.

'He's as good as gold, Ginger,' Ernie informed me in a stage whisper. I nodded back with discreet thanks.

I began to make my weekend farewell to Sergeant Griffiths. 'Okay, sarge, I'll see you on Mon –' A dramatic yell from Ernie cut me short in mid-sentence.

'Look out, Arfur! The law!'

Arfur was incredible. He threw everything – slips, book, pencil and cash – into the air and turned on his toes and ran. It wasn't even an ordinary run, he was down that street like a greased whippet.

Now Taff Griffiths may have been advancing in years and a stone or two overweight, but he still played rugby quite regularly and was really quite fit. Once he realized that Arthur was legging it, he was off in hot pursuit. The main problem with this hot pursuit was the manner in which it was carried out. Taff had a most peculiar style of running, not unlike that of an ostrich. Keeping an ugly upright stance, he splayed out his great flat, cumbersome feet and covered ground at an enormous rate. As effective as this sprinting was, the sight of it always made me dissolve into fits of uncontrollable laughter.

As the runners reached the end of the road, Arthur made to turn right, which would have taken him into the next street and out of our sight. Sizing up the situation, Ernie came to an instant decision. In a very loud voice he called, 'ALL RIGHT, ARFUR, LET 'IM 'AVE YER!' The effect on Arthur was instantaneous. One moment he had been running flat out, the next he had stopped dead. There had been no slowing-down process, it was completely instant.

Unfortunately for Arthur, Taff had by now closed the gap between them to just a few feet. Launching himself at the fleeing youth, he struck him waist-high just at the split second that Arthur had braked to a halt. This ferocious rugby-tackle caused them both to crash into a cluster of dustbins and rubbish bags that had stood passively on the street corner. Lids, egg-shells, potato-peelings and ashes suddenly spewed out over the pavement. Lying among them like two panting lovers were the puzzled Arthur and the furious sergeant.

I was laughing so much I could scarcely draw breath. Eventually I recovered enough to turn to the perplexed bookmaker. 'Ernie, what the bloody hell was that all about?'

He shook his head in bewilderment. 'I'm sorry, guv', I just fort I'd make it look real. I didn't fink the prat would run like that, though.'

'Oh, it looked real right enough,' I agreed, 'although I'm not sure which "prat" you're talking about. There's not much between either of them.'

Sergeant Emlyn Roland Griffiths held his prisoner by the arm as he shrugged off the remnants of the Chrysell Road rubbish. His trousers were ripped at both knees and he had a sizeable graze on his chin. He was also furious. Arthur had fared little better. His nose bled profusely and he limped badly on one foot.

'Did it look all right, Ern?' he asked nervously.

'It's all right, Taff, he was trying to make it "look real",' I explained. 'Ernie thought it would be a good idea.'

Taff said nothing but looked thoughtfully down to his flapping trousers.

'I'll tell yer what,' broke in Ernie, now desperate to please. 'Let's go into the King's 'Ead and while we're 'aving a drink p'raps old Cyril will let yer clean up a bit.'

I was still having difficulty in suppressing the giggles as Taff and Arthur disappeared into the pub lavatory to tend to their wounds. Cyril the landlord pulled up four foaming pints. 'It's all right, Ernie,' he said, raising his hand. 'These are on me. That was the best entertainment in this street since the war.'

The two casualties eventually reappeared, sharing the friendship of souls in distress. I made a lukewarm offer to accompany Taff back to the station but by then he was on his second pint and becoming more tolerant by the minute. I had a wedding to attend and Ernie had a business to run. We said our goodbyes at the door and arranged to meet at the court on Monday morning. We had left Taff and Arthur sitting at the bar, which was where they remained until closing time. I can only imagine what they looked like by the time they reached the police station some two and a half hours later.

I did not see either of the participants again until we reassembled at court on Monday. Far from clearing up, the wounds of both of them had worsened. Arthur had sustained a badly sprained ankle and wore a plaster cast and walked with a stick. Poor Taff's chin had turned septic and looked like an early stage of leprosy. Although the case went smoothly enough – a quick guilty plea and a seven-pound fine – I sensed that Ernie was anything but happy.

'All right, Ern?' I asked dutifully. 'It all turned out all right in the end, eh?'

'No, I've not seen either of them since Saturday. Three-quarters of an hour before closing time, they popped out of the pub and put on a ten-quid bet with me.'

'Ten quid! They must have been mad, it must have been all the money they had!'

'It was, they were so pissed that at first I wouldn't take it,' announced Ernie nobly. 'Then I fort, well I'll keep 'em 'appy, like – so I took it.'

'And?'

'The shits backed Sundew. It won at twenty-five to bleedin' one!'

Although this was not the most distressing news I had ever heard, I felt that I should at least offer my condolences.

'Oh, I'm sorry about –'

'Sorry? Sorry?' he echoed. 'I'll tell yer what, Ginger, that's the last bleedin' stick-up I'm ever arranging. In future I'll get nicked meself! It'll be a bloody sight cheaper!'

10. Warrant officer

I had been in the force six years when the subject of promotion raised its head. Sam Parry had moved on and the new superintendent was very keen that his men should be ambitious. 'Hullo, Cole! Sitting for the exam this year, are we?' was his customary greeting. This was all very well but there was more to it than that. Firstly, I had to decide if promotion was really worth the effort. If one was simply going to remain a sergeant, then undoubtedly it was not. Unfortunately one had to become a sergeant before becoming anything else. There was obviously something to be said for being a Trenchard-Boy!

Being a sergeant had never appealed to me in the slightest. In those days before the huge civilian admin units, sergeants did about ninety-five per cent of the station paperwork. They were unquestionably the hardest working section of the force. For this enormous workload plus a great deal of responsibility, they received around twenty-five shillings a week more than the average PC. In addition to this, there was the problem of where one should be posted to after promotion. Would the area be too much of a contrast? My own station, Carter Street, was a typical grotty inner-city manor, where one could see and experience most of life's tribulations. It should have prepared a young constable for service almost anywhere in London. But after six years in Southwark, how would I adjust to a more salubrious area, say Belgravia or Hampstead?

In this needless worry, I had been greatly influenced by the dismay of an enthusiastic new sergeant who arrived on our manor from semi-rural Keston. There his most dramatic task had been to round up runaway ponies from the gypsy encampment. For the sake of ambition he had given up this country life. In exchange for his green fields and tranquillity, we offered him some of the worst slums in London and a crime rate of 10,000 a year.

He took one look at our grimy building with its crowded yard and packed cells and almost ran weeping back to Keston. The problem was not just confined to the police station. He found the whole area a totally different way of life. Take parking, for instance. This can be a problem in many urban areas but at Carter Street there was an additional hazard – pigeons. These are not just ordinary pigeons, oh no. They are more akin to loose-bowelled eagles. The railway that runs across the station yard is built on a series of arches which in turn are infested with these birds. It is like a gigantic aviary. On the morning the new sergeant arrived, he could not believe his good fortune. There, not thirty feet from the station entrance, was a clear parking spot. He eased his car under the railway bridge and entered the building. His first big mistake.

Almost before he had turned his back, the pigeons sent out what we at the station called their 'path finder'. This is a fat old cooing waddler, who can splatter a speeding windscreen from a height of sixty feet. Once this first attack has been pressed home, any car under that bridge is fair game for every dysentery-racked bird in south London.

At the end of his first day as station officer, he had dealt with twenty-two charges, two complaints against policemen, the annual visit by the auditors and a station cleaner who had fallen down the stairs. He had not had time to eat, drink or even go to the lavatory. Having staggered punch-drunk from the station, all he wanted was to get home as soon as possible. Firstly though he would need to dig out his car.

'Whatever is that?' he exclaimed.

'*That* is pigeon shit, sarge,' he was informed.

'I've never seen pigeon shit like it,' he cried in disbelief.

'I don't suppose you've seen pigeons like 'em either. You never want to park under the bridge, sarge. It'll put hours on your day.'

Within a week the new sergeant had made a decision. He would apply to revert back to constable. This was not as simple as he at first thought. First, someone else was rounding up the ponies and had no plans to relinquish the task to become Commissioner. Secondly, if he had met disaster on his promotion to sergeant, there was no guarantee he would not meet it again on his reversion to PC. He therefore decided to stay and fight. 'Fighting' in this case was studying for the next rank. Carter Street is a bit like that, it provides a great incentive to move.

This, then, was my problem. I could never see myself as senior officer material. I lacked both the application and the maturity. I enjoyed being a policeman immensely, probably because I never took it very seriously. This was, after all, a regular and justifiable criticism made of me by numerous inspectors. I therefore decided quite early in my service that promotion was not for me. In addition, I actually liked the confounded station!

However, liking it was one thing; spending the rest of my service there was quite another. I began to explore the possibility of trying something else besides street-duty. This problem was eventually solved for me by an invitation I discovered in *Police Orders*. This publication is an internal bi-weekly that contains changes in legislation, promotion lists and such like. It stated that a register was to be made of suitable applicants for relieving duty in London courts. In the first instance men would relieve on a temporary basis, then, if they were found to be suitable, a permanent position would be offered, as and when vacancies occurred. This appealed to me greatly. First, there was the variety offered by relieving at the different courts; second, there was no night-duty!

The disadvantage was that I knew absolutely nothing

about the workings of the court. I soon discovered that the job was split into two groups: warrant officers and gaolers. Warrant officers mainly dealt with the outside work, such as routine court enquiries, and arresting the occasional fine-defaulters. The work was interesting and rich with characters. Gaolers, on the other hand, worked inside the courts and rarely ventured out. The forbidding name 'gaoler' was something of a misnomer because only part of the work was to do with locking up prisoners.

Unlike my application for traffic patrol, I was accepted for the list without even an interview. My first attachment was to the Newington rating court. This rather grandly named department did not operate from a court at all, but from a church hall-cum-youth club in Kennington. At least it was a church hall and youth club on six days a week, but each Friday it became a court. On that day there would be a chaotic hour as the ping-pong tables were put away and the toilet cleaned. Space was at a premium. Chairs would be crowded together to face the tiny stage on which the most comfortable chairs would be placed for the lay bench of magistrates, usually three or four in number. This bench would hear cases where distress warrants had been ordered for non-payment of rates and other civil matters.

Although the system worked reasonably well, there was one great disadvantage to seating the court in this hall. One of the more regular members of the bench was a titled, tweed-suited lady from Chelsea. Now any sitting female in a tight skirt on a raised stage is going to experience difficulties at the best of times but this one had an additional problem. Although no great beauty, she did have the most magnificent pair of thighs. Many a witness lost all track of his carefully rehearsed defence when m'Lady readjusted her position by recrossing her legs.

The solicitors for prosecution and defence sat in a row immediately in front of this stage. I found it of particular interest to study the reaction of newcomers. Court solicitors as a general rule like it to seem that they are questioning the witnesses from memory. This is rubbish, of course, and just part of their act. Few of them even look at the papers until five minutes before a case starts. Their copy of the witness's statement usually lies on the table in front of them. By peering beneath their spectacles and tracing with a pencil or finger, they can, almost imperceptibly, compare his replies to his original statement. Nearly every lawyer will glance at the bench from time to time to assess the impact he is making. This is particularly prevalent after scoring a strong legal point. In order to do this, he will need to make a smooth visual movement from witness, via bench, down to the all-important line on the statement. With a little practice they do it very well. It is essential, however, that this movement is accomplished in an unruffled manner. A slight falter, or a momentary loss of place, can ruin the whole effect. There is no margin for error. Yet time and time again, experienced lawyers were reduced to open-mouthed stares by the flash of a suspendered thigh.

After I had covered at the court for almost two weeks, the court sergeant told me we were to have a 'big case'. In addition to the usual solicitors and lawyers, we were to have counsel present. I became quite excited, wondering what it could be. Anything would be better than the dreary cases I had seen so far. I obviously realized that it would be nothing too dramatic; after all, we only dealt with local-government offences. Still, there was always a chance that a celebrity brothel had failed to pay its rates. Extra chairs were crowded into the front row and eventually three expensive-looking briefcased gentlemen made their way into the hall.

The newcomers sat down and there, on the table in front of the fattest of them, was a small, clear, plastic bag. Inside this bag was the most hideous sight I had ever seen. Try as I might, I could not begin to decipher what it was. It appeared to be a growth of some description. It was a particularly horrible green in colour and about the size of an average man's fist. Although it did not actually pulsate, I felt that it ought to have done. Small trickles of liquid ran from it and droplets, presumably of the same liquid, were festooned all over the inside of the bag. It looked like something Frankenstein kept in a jar. Should it ever escape, I felt, we would all be in great peril. The whole thing looked utterly evil.

Shuddering, I whispered to the court sergeant, 'What on earth is that?'

'It's the "big case", lad,' he hissed. 'That's why all the big-wigs are here today.'

'Yes, I gathered that,' I squeaked. 'But what is in the bag? Is it someone's hand?'

He stared at me puzzled. 'Someone's hand?' he echoed. 'No, you silly sod. It's a salmon roll!'

'Salmon roll!'

'Shssssssh, here come the bench.' He turned to the court in general. 'All rise!' he boomed.

The fat counsel's eyebrows raised as Her Ladyship walked towards her chair. She sat down and bounced into position a couple of times. He reached quickly for his spectacles.

'Black,' murmured the sergeant dreamily.

'Pardon?' I asked.

'Black, she's got black suspenders on today.' He moaned in mock ecstasy. 'Last week they were white and she looked virginal, but I much prefer black, it makes her look dirty. I have this fantasy about being her kept man.' He sighed a very long sigh. 'Oh those thighs, those thighs, I could die happily between them.'

'You probably would,' I observed. 'I think she could crack coconuts with them.'

Almost as if she had heard, the lady looked across the room towards us. She gave a wide smile. 'Yes, sergeant?' At first I think the sergeant actually believed he was receiving his call. 'Are we ready, sergeant?'

The penny finally dropped. 'Oh, yes, ma'am, yes,' he stammered. 'Er – case number one, Your Worships. This is an offence under section two of the Food and Drugs Act of 1957. Southwark Council versus Messrs Blenkinsop, Blaggett and Haverdean . . .'

The curtain had finally risen on our big case. I was agog, and convinced that the sergeant had lied about the salmon roll.

In effect he had told the absolute truth. The reason for everyone's presence that Friday morning was just one solitary salmon roll. Or rather, the rusty nail that nestled inside it. Bert Simpson, a labourer at Blenkinsop's tin-plate factory, had purchased a salmon roll with his cup of tea in the firm's canteen some three months earlier. Having bitten generously into it, Bert had been rather surprised when his top-set had cracked upon an inch-and-a-quarter flooring nail. He had returned the roll to the canteen, where the manageress, a vigorous, tight-bodied blonde named Celia, had not treated his complaint with the gravity Bert thought it merited.

Sid Russell, a friend of Bert's and definitely not a friend of anyone else's, suggested that Bert should take his teeth, roll and nail along to the local town hall. Armed with Sid's advice, Bert sought out the Public Health Inspector during his lunchbreak. That gentleman promptly confiscated the roll and set the wheels in motion that would take Messrs Blenkinsop, Blaggett and Haverdean to the Newington rating court. Not to be outdone, Messrs Blenkinsop, Blaggett and Haverdean then took the small chain of Richardson's Bakeries to court with them. Richardson's agreed that they made the roll, but that the flour was purchased from Nightingale's, a local mill. All three firms, being limited companies, were then required to be represented by counsel. To provide a continuity of evidence, the case required that Bert, Celia, Sid, the Public Health Inspector, representatives from each firm and three expensive counsel, should spend an entire Friday morning in our church hall, seeing that justice was done. As indeed it was. The tight-bummed, wiggling Celia provided the court with at least some distraction from Her Ladyship's thighs and the subsequent fine of ten pounds on Nightingale's Mills seemed to satisfy honour all round.

Fascinating though the interlude had been, I felt I could hardly spend the next twenty years looking up Her Ladyship's skirt, so I was quite happy to leave the sergeant to his fantasies and receive my next temporary posting.

Lambeth Magistrates' Court was a typical busy inner-city court. It was a small, pokey little building, crowded with policemen, solicitors, prisoners and anxious relatives. All such courts build up to a daily peak of sheer unbridled turmoil. Shortly after eight o'clock the first of the overnight prisoners are delivered from surrounding police stations. These are soon followed by others from remand centres and borstals. Just before ten o'clock, those on bail will report to the gaoler's office. These are rapidly followed by arresting officers, witnesses, defence and prosecution solicitors. The bell on the telephone plays counter-melody to the bell on the security door as each vies for attention.

'Who's on the bench today?' 'How much did I have on me?' 'How long d'you reckon I'll get?' The same three questions are heard over and over again.

One of the first tasks of the assistant gaoler is to 'get-up' the prisoners. That is, to assemble them all in the waiting room next to the courtroom. Usually the prisoner does not know anyone else except the officer who arrested him. This can frequently lead to a strange camaraderie between the two. The hardest 'nut' from the night before can become the world's greatest 'grass' in the minutes preceding his appearance in the dock. Often the most determined intended 'not guilty' plea will be reversed on the basis of this new-found friendship.

The overriding problem for any gaoler is the smell. Such a smell! In an effort to reduce it to manageable proportions, drunk cases are absolutely raced through.

Once the court is sitting, the voice of the gaoler will boom out every two minutes as each drunk is placed before the magistrate.

'McNeil!'

The permanent smell of stale bodies and dried urine hangs heavily on the centrally heated air. The smell of a 'mether' or 'wino' threads its way through the service of every street copper.

'Fitzpatrick!'

The grizzled faces, the stubbly beards, the trousers stiff with dirt.

'Ryan!'

The bloodshot eyes, the croaking accents.

'Callaghan!'

Sometimes, though, when they reached Callaghan, the gaolers at Lambeth would falter a little. With the names Callaghan and Gallaghan on the list, they had once had good reason to falter.

'We must keep them well separate or we'll be in dead trouble this morning,' the gaoler had said. He led the first of them towards the courtroom. 'Which one are you?'

'–allaghan, sir.'

'Who?'

'–allaghan, sir.'

'Hmmm. How do you spell it, then?' asked the gaoler, determined to get it right.

'I don't know, sir,' said –allaghan confidentially. 'You see, it's an alias.' Conversations with drunks can be confusing even when they are sober.

The first few days at Lambeth filled me with dismay. Everybody was so busy during the mid-morning rush that I could never see them having sufficient time to teach me the job. People would certainly tell me what to do but never *why* it was done. My blackest moment came when I answered the telephone in the gaoler's office.

'I want to speak to Chick Robinson urgently,' said a distant voice.

I placed my palm over the handset. 'Who's Chick Robinson, sarge?' I asked the sergeant gaoler.

'He's in court at the moment. What is it?'

'Someone wants him urgent.'

'Well, that's okay, just tiptoe into court and tell him.'

Now some people tiptoe around courts all day and no one takes a blind bit of notice. Yet whenever I attempt it, my shoes squeak. They never squeak at any other time, just in court. The defence stopped speaking and His Worship cast me a withering glance. I was tiptoeing so lightly that I found myself holding my breath. By the time I reached the ear of Chick Robinson, I was so breathless I could hardly speak.

'Phone,' I panted.

'What about it?' responded Chick, puzzled.

'You're . . . wanted . . . on . . . it,' I wheezed.

By this time all dialogue in the court had totally ceased.

'Thanks,' said Chick, thrusting his clipboard in my hand. 'Just look after this, I won't be long.'

'But what do I do?' A note of terror had crept into my voice.

'Nothing, nothing at all. This case will take another half-hour at least. I'll be back inside two minutes. Just stand there and look knowledgeable.'

'Is it all right with you, officer, if we continue?' asked the magistrate irritably. I swallowed hard and responded with a weak smile.

He turned once more to the defence solicitor. 'Carry on, Mr Daventry.'

'Well, Your Worship, on the basis of that submission, I would like to ask for at least six weeks' remand – on bail, of course,' submitted Mr Daventry.

'Hmmmm, yes, I see.' The magistrate rubbed his chin thoughtfully. He then leaned forward and shared a muffled conversation with the clerk of the court. 'Very well, Mr Daventry, six weeks it is, then.'

Peering over his glasses, His Worship looked directly at

me. I felt, and doubtless looked, quite blank.

'Yes, officer?' he asked, expectantly.

'Sir?' I bleated.

'The date, the date. What date can you give us?'

By then I had realized that I was supposed to furnish the court with the date of the resumed hearing, six weeks hence. Me! I didn't even know the date of that very day! I looked panic-stricken at the clipboard. There must have been a dozen sheets of paper attached. I released the clip and every one of them slipped smoothly and instantly to the floor. In all of my life I have never been closer to tears.

'Mr Weekes!' exclaimed the magistrate. 'Can *you* do something?'

Weekes was the court inspector who had been sitting quietly at his desk doubtless wishing I was dead.

'Er –' began Weekes, rising in response.

Suddenly the door to the office opened and Chick glided back into the court. I could have kissed him.

'What's he want, Ginger?' he whispered.

'He wants a remand date for six weeks' time,' I whimpered.

'Is that all?' He picked up three of the sheets and glanced at two of them for no more than a few seconds. 'How about Thursday 27th April, Your Worship?'

'Thank you, officer. Will that suit you, Mr Daventry?'

'It will indeed, sir.'

Breathing a sigh of relief, I decided to keep my head down and pick up the remainder of the papers. Unfortunately they had slid across the highly polished floor. As I began to rummage, I found Chick Robinson crouching alongside me.

'Ginger,' he hissed.

'Yeh?'

'Piss off!'

Of all the instructions and requests given to me that morning, that was the first one I had understood. I was out of the court within seconds.

'How would you like to work in the warrant office for the rest of your stint here?' asked the sergeant gaoler later that morning. 'As it's only for a couple of weeks, perhaps we can work something out.'

'Sure, sarge, sure.' I had already decided that a gaoler's office was not for me. 'Cannot work under pressure' was doubtless emblazoned on my progress report.

I must say that I took to the change very well. I enjoyed the greater freedom and the characters that I met. At times I was even successful, never more so than on my very first day, or, more accurately, evening. Winston Stanley Brown had moved into the area from Cardiff, where he had rather 'forgotten' a fine of £600. There were at least eight other black males at Winston's address, and Winston had never once come to light on previous enquiries or even searches. No one in the warrant office had even the vaguest idea of what he looked like, and there was no doubt that he was giving the whole department a runaround.

Warrant officers usually work singly and in plain clothes and are issued with an easily recognized briefcase. These cases were not, however, given to trainees such as myself, which presented me with a slight problem. Numerous case-papers were essential to the job and one did need a means of carrying them. The object that I owned nearest to a briefcase was a square, squat composite box, picked up long ago on a trip by my grandfather. It had long ago lost its handle and was now held together by string. I had used it to store old football programmes. Suitably equipped, I borrowed my father's prewar Austin and set out on my first calls as a warrant officer.

The formidable list of fruitless calls made previously at Winston Brown's address appeared in the margin of the case-papers. My first reaction was to save time and drive straight past. Changing my mind, I decided to give 97 Batten Road a quick visit. My knock was answered by an enormous black woman.

'Yes?'

'Mr Brown, please, Winston Stanley.'

'Ah yes, come in.'

I was a little taken aback at this hospitality. The only way access had been gained previously was via a search warrant. She led me into a rather pleasant but overfurnished sitting-room.

'Sit yourself down please, I'll fetch him.'

I slipped into a comfortable chair and placed my string-bound box on my lap. She turned back towards the door and called loudly up the staircase.

'Winston!'

There was a moment's pause then back came the reply. 'Yes, what is it?'

'Winston, it's the doctor, honey.'

Doctor! I glanced down at the case. My thoughts raced, what do I do now? She was obviously expecting the doctor. God only knows what sort of doctor she thought carried his instruments in an old box. Heavy footsteps descended the staircase. Seconds later a giant entered the room. He was colossal! I just hoped he was friendly.

'Good evening, sir,' he greeted.

'Evening,' I responded. 'Mr Brown?'

'That's me, sir.'

'Winston Stanley?'

He faltered slightly and glanced quickly at the woman. 'Yeh, yeh that's me sure enough.'

'Mr Brown,' I swallowed hard. 'I'm afraid I have here a warrant for your arrest for non-payment of a six-hundred-pound fine, imposed on you a year ago in Cardiff.'

'But you're a doctor!' interrupted the woman. 'Or are you a police doctor?' she added, her eyes narrowing.

'No, love, I'm not a doctor, far from it. I'm a policeman from the warrant office at Lambeth Magistrates' Court.'

Winston Stanley Brown rose to his huge feet and walked menacingly across the room. Ignoring me, he leaned over the now seated woman and placed his right index finger just under her nose.

118

'Letilda, how come you let this officer into this house?'

'Well, he's got a case like all doctors have,' she protested.

Leaving his finger in position, he glanced quickly at grandfather's old box. 'A case? That's a doctor's case?' He punctuated every word by pushing the tip of Letilda's nose.

He then turned his attention to me. 'This warrant you talk about, will I have to go to prison?'

'You would certainly have to go to a police station until tomorrow morning, then it would be up to the magistrate to decide the next move.'

'How about if I paid the money?'

'Well, he would doubtless release you. It's the money they really want, not you.'

'I mean *now*. Supposin' I paid it now?'

'Winston! Where would you get that kind of money now?' asked the woman, very close to tears.

'Shut up, Letilda, you've done enough damage for one day.'

'Well, I'd give you a receipt and that would be it, I suppose.' In truth I had no idea what the situation was. I had just not expected £600 so easily. I therefore had not clarified the position before I left the office.

He ambled over to a large chipped china dog that stood eyeless by the fireplace. He tipped it up and removed a plug of rolled-up newspapers from its base. He slipped in his fingers and just as quickly withdrew them with a fat roll of bank notes.

'Winston!' shrieked the woman. 'How long has that been there?'

'Ever since I was fined. I kept it there just in case.'

He counted out a hundred and twenty extremely dirty five-pound notes. I gave him a receipt and bade him goodnight.

Next morning in the office, the sergeant in charge asked me how I had managed with my first round of calls.

'Only one result, sarge,' I answered, as off-handedly as possible.

'An arrest?'

'No, he paid.'

He reached for the paying-in register. 'How much was it, Ginger?'

I gave an exaggerated yawn. 'How about six hundred quid, sarge?'

His eyes instantly lit up. 'Brown! You nicked Winston Brown?'

'Nope, I didn't need to nick him, he just paid up like a good 'un.'

'We've been after him for months! Did you have any trouble?'

'Nah, you just have to know how to treat him. Simply sounded his chest, took his temperature and he was putty in my hands.'

I enjoyed warrant-office work; in addition, I was lucky at it. Eventually, I suppose, I might have become one. The drawback was that under the list system there was no way of ensuring which department or even which court one would be posted to. The deciding factor for me was my posting to the gaoler's office at Balham. This was a small basement area about the size of a good rabbit-hutch. I had arrived for work on a wet July morning around seven o'clock. As I left for home just before four in the afternoon, I slipped on my raincoat and climbed the stairs to ground level. As I opened the door to the street, I reeled back from the glaring sun. Everywhere were girls in summer dresses and fellows in shirtsleeves. It had been a perfect July day and I had not even been aware of it. It was then I realized that I could never spend the next twenty years with such uncertainty. I knew that I needed the streets. Okay, so I was not going to specialize or sit for promotion. What, then? Can one really spend thirty years pounding a beat? Well I had enjoyed it so far, that was for sure. On that basis I decided to let matters take their own course.

I resigned from the list and joined my old relief back at the station the following Monday. Monday night, to be precise – bloody night-duty. Perhaps I had been just a wee bit hasty . . . ?

11. Star maker?

In my off-duty time I had become more and more involved with youth club work, or rather one aspect of it. As a thirteen-year-old I had joined Charterhouse Boys' Club and remained with them throughout my teens. After leaving the army I had progressed to the 'Old Boys' where we had formed a very successful football team. About twenty of us met weekly in the club building and used their facilities for training. One evening it was pointed out to me by Bert Nolan, the club leader, that we were getting a great deal out of the club but putting nothing back in.

'What is it you want, then?' I asked, rather touchily.

'Well, you're a keen enough footballer. If you could just take some youngsters for training it would be a help.'

He was right, of course, he usually was. We were all grown men and each Monday we would happily kick each other all around the gym and, having paid our subscriptions, leave the place with perfectly clear consciences. The more I thought about Bert's idea, the more it appealed to me. I was playing at least three games of football each week and I was convinced I had a great deal of expertise to offer. I had visions of becoming a crack coach.

I could see it quite clearly. A sparkling new tracksuit and a dozen attentive kids, each devouring the pearls of soccer wisdom that fell from my lips. First, though, as a non-smoker, I would need to buy a pipe. All good football coaches at that time smoked pipes. Once I had a pipe *and* a new tracksuit I would work on the image. Perhaps in some dramatic cup-final I would watch the match in silence for the first-half, quietly sucking on my old briar. Just before half-time I would spot the solitary flaw in the opposition. During the interval teamtalk, I would explain my plan in a quiet, unemotional manner by using the pipe stem. In the second half, of course, my team would romp home, clear winners. Solely on the basis of my perception. Later, as the team lifted the trophy they so richly deserved, the quiet, unassuming coach would fade modestly into the background with his beloved pipe.

It was a truly great dream but it did have flaws, the first of them being that no matter how hard I tried, the rotten pipe would never stay alight for more than a few moments. The only exception to this rule was when I was convinced it was extinguished and it burnt a hole in my coat. The irony was that the pipe was totally unnecessary. My carefully researched theories would have been just as ignored if I had been lying drunk on the touchline.

All that had happened was that I had discovered the first problem that besets all coaches, namely the players! Not one footballer in a hundred considers that his game needs improving. That overweight, squat-legged, teenaged oaf who falls over each time he touches the ball is convinced that he is not playing for England purely because he has never had the breaks. The coach knows that the only break he really needs is to his neck. I soon learned that to coach teenagers well, one must yield a big stick. 'You do that once more, Danny, and you are out! D'you hear me? O-U-T – OUT.' This is the time when a coach is thankful that 'out' is a three-letter word. Few footballers would understand it if it had five.

The gymnasium at Charterhouse measures about 75 feet by 35 feet. On an average training evening some eighteen youngsters would attend. On a few occasions we had twenty-eight of them. Each player would then have an area to himself about the size of a good table. Just to increase the problem, the walls were splattered with iron radiators, protruding hot-water pipes and, frequently, blood. It wasn't so much a soccer coach the club needed, more a bone surgeon. This compressed aggression would usually erupt into at least one stand-up fight. Sometimes half a dozen. It was then that I first threw off my mantle of a quiet, fair-minded, pipe-smoking soccer philosopher. Instead I became a screaming, ranting, shirt-pulling belligerent, who was at least in with chances. After two hours of this war-like, sudden-death football, condensation would stream down the walls and lie in lakes on the floor. Just one more hazard for the boiling players.

These evenings had their rewards, however. They bred a player who, if he wanted the ball at all, had to fight like hell to get it. That, plus the astonishing flair of Bert Nolan, the club leader, enabled the club to win every one of the London Federation of Boys' Clubs soccer trophies in the same season: under-nineteens, under-seventeens, under-fifteens, and under-thirteens. It was a feat never performed before in the entire history of the Federation.

Bert amazed me. He had a way with youngsters that I never saw equalled. Boys who invariably disobeyed their own parents would wait on his every wish. He gave trust and responsibility where none before had existed. Boys who would readily steal their grandmother's pension were regularly trusted with the club takings. Not a penny went astray. His ability to talk freely to youngsters without ever appearing patronizing was a very high skill.

The Charterhouse door was open all hours. Christmas Day could find a dozen kids kicking a football in the gym. Others might gather around to listen to one of Bert's stories, perhaps of his old war wound. (Actually he was too young for the war and he was really suffering from rheumatism; still, the kids were impressed.)

Bert had a remarkable knowledge of many subjects – football, swimming, rock-climbing, motorcycle maintenance and, surprisingly, card-playing. One group of eighteen-year-olds once decided to indulge in an all-night poker game. Bert advised strongly against it. His advice was, unusually, rejected. Working on the if-I-can't-fight-them-then-I'll-join-them basis, he sat in the game. The boys left just before dawn, downcast and broke. They had learned a valuable lesson and he had made a reasonable profit.

This short indulgence was very rare, though. Mostly he would dip into his own pocket to provide some necessity, or even small luxury, to an unfortunate lad. I learned from Bert Nolan the one essential ingredient for any successful boys' club. It was the leader. We were lucky, we had the best.

By this time I had become so involved with the club that I applied to attend a residential FA coaching course. I was to fail this first attempt miserably. A year or two later I successfully took another, this time at the newly opened sports centre at Crystal Palace in south London. Until that weekend I had always considered myself a football fanatic. My first doubts appeared when we were led out on a pitch at six in the morning, in a thick September mist. We had not even been permitted a cup of tea!

If I thought that the acquisition of a coaching badge would smooth my relationship with the more difficult players, then I should have known better. A badge does little for a coach other than decorate his tracksuit. Influence is bestowed by the personality of the coach and by nothing else.

By this time I had begun to widen my scope. In addition to training youngsters in the gym, I began to manage two of the Saturday teams. The average age of both sides was around nineteen. This caused me no little problem at the police station. One can hardly manage a football team without actually *being* there. But I was, after all, still a policeman, and Saturdays are an extremely busy day. However, with a great deal of conniving, scheming, cooperation and luck, I missed just three Saturdays in fifteen seasons!

If I had found coaching difficult, there were times when managing was almost impossible. At Charterhouse we were unquestionably a very successful side. Most young players in such a team, particularly if they are playing well themselves, will consider there is little that a coach can teach them.

None illustrated this better than Frankie Downs, a ferocious little battler who would average thirty goals a season. Although stockily built, Frankie was the smallest footballer I had ever seen, but he played with the tenacity of Attila. Frankie would be 'sent off' on average three times each season. If neither opponents nor referee knew him, then I would give him a fictitious name, preferably one he could spell. The problem with this ruse, however, was that once met, always remembered. There was no way we could repeat this trick against the same opponents.

Frankie was no respecter of size, and when he was sent off it would usually be for fighting with a defender at least fifteen inches taller than he was. Whenever this happened I would request a personal hearing. Frankie would arrive at the discipline enquiry wearing his thick-lensed spectacles and barely visible alongside the Goliath who had fought with him. The committees never seemed to fathom how this inoffensive midget could cause such mayhem. Despite the number of times he was sent off, he served just two comparatively short suspensions. I would spend hours persuading him to control his temper and I honestly believe he did try. But as soon as the first tackle was made on his whirring little legs, he would be up throwing punches. His temper, however, was not Frankie's only drawback. Excellent footballer though he was, he was little more than a passenger for the first fifteen minutes of any match. This was because he would be crouched on the touchline having what the rest of the team would inelegantly call 'a real good spew'. This was not caused by nerves, or a debilitating hereditary complaint. It was caused by pie-and-mash.

Each Saturday lunchtime, shortly before the team met, Frankie could be found in Manzie's pie-and-mash shop polishing off two large pies and a plateful of mash. Now pie-and-mash is most excellent fare, half the population of south London is raised upon it, and Manzie's pies in particular are above reproach. However, it is a food that can lie on the chest like grapeshot and is best digested during a half-hour doze in an armchair. Unfortunately Frankie worked most Saturday mornings and possessed a rather keen appetite. His route from his office to the club took him past Manzie's tantalizing open doorway. The aroma was something he could never resist, it was as simple as that. No matter how many times we pleaded with him, his resistance would always collapse. Sixteen minutes into every match, therefore, having regurgitated the last of Manzie's pastry, he would give a good cough and hurl himself back into the fray. Two minutes later, as fit as a fiddle, he would probably be in a fight.

With two teams to manage, there was not only Frankie to contend with. I also had to find common ground with some of my other youngsters. With a pool of some twenty-five south London teenagers, it was a certainty that a sizeable minority of them would be into some sort of trouble with the law. These offences ranged from unlicensed street-trading to murder! If I was to have any credibility with the lads at all, I knew I had to forget that I was a policeman. Of course it wasn't just I who had to forget it, they had to forget it too. The amazing aspect of it all was that they did. I could certainly have carved out a whole constabulary career for myself on the information I learned in those changing rooms. Trust, however, was complete on both sides.

The murder, of course, was something rather different. I had arranged a pre-season training session on a sunny August Saturday afternoon. I arrived at the park suitably clad in shorts, tracktop and trainers and clutching two footballs. About twenty of my players were awaiting my arrival, sprawled out on the grass outside the changing rooms. This was a customary scene. Park-keepers are notoriously reluctant to let these premises to any rough-looking bunch until they see someone whom they can consider a 'responsible person'. My appearance, therefore, was the signal for 'Wally-the-parky' to open up. At first I neither saw nor heard anything in the behaviour of the players to indicate that anything unusual had taken place. There was the usual dressing-room banter. Someone had forgotten his shorts, another his boots, while the team's hypochondriac had just discovered a new ailment. 'D'you reckon this is athlete's foot?' 'No, it's leprosy,' he was assured.

'Al,' one of the more thoughtful players called across. (For some reason most of the team referred to me by that name.)

I returned an enquiring glance.

'Jimmy Beaton won't be 'ere today. 'E's been nicked. Oh,' he added as an afterthought, 'so has Micky Barnes.'

'Blast!' I complained. After training I had intended to split the group into two even sides for a practice match. With two forwards incarcerated in the local police station, this would leave me with an abundance of defenders. 'What've they been nicked for?'

'Murder, I fink,' he announced as he calmly laced up his trainers.

'What!!'

'Yeh, Billy Summers got done in last night and the law reckons Jimmy Beaton did it.'

After a brief series of questions I discovered that the three named lads had been at a party the night before. Micky Barnes had thrown a punch at someone and a fight had started. Billy Summers had wound up dead. 'But Jimmy and Billy have *always* fought each other, but never *seriously*,' I said.

My informant just shrugged. My observation was true, though. Bill Summers and Jim Beaton were almost inseparable, but they also fought like cat and dog. They would argue incessantly about anything and everything. Only a few weeks earlier, Billy had broken his own wrist by banging Jimmy on the head during an argument on the

128

snooker table. To the best of my knowledge Billy's forearm was still in plaster. They would black each other's eyes quite cheerfully, but murder? Never! I had always made a point of never becoming involved in my players' escapades but I knew I could not sit on the fence with this one.

A few minutes later I called at the enquiry desk at the local police station. My first piece of luck was knowing the sergeant on duty there. I had played football both with and against him many times.

'Hullo, Ginger! Fancy dress, are we?'

I glanced quickly down at my appearance. I had completely forgotten that I was dressed for a training stint at the park.

'Have you got two of my players in here for murder?'

'Oh, so they're your bloody players, are they? Having seen you play I'm not surprised.' He lifted the flap and invited me into the office. 'Come through, I'll taken you up to see the DI.'

'Have they charged them yet, Jack?' I asked.

'Charged them?' he exclaimed. 'Good God, no! It'll be ages before that happens. We've got all our cells full of youngsters from that party. I think the guv'nor's still trying to sort out who's who.'

A podgy, red-faced, middle-aged man with thinning hair was in the process of pouring himself a large scotch.

'This is PC Cole here, guv', from Carter Street.' The detective inspector cast a quick quizzical eye over my blue nylon shorts. 'Well, that is to say he usually is from Carter Street. Today he's a football coach. He knows two of your prime suspects very well. He's called in to see if he can help.'

Turning down the detective's offer of an equally large scotch, I added but briefly to the sergeant's introduction. The detective inspector seemed genuinely glad to see me and suggested that I went into the cells and persuaded Beaton and Barnes to cooperate. So far, apart from strenuous denials, they had said nothing.

'Well I'll do what I can,' I promised. 'But I'll tell you one thing, guv'. There is absolutely no way that Jimmy Beaton would ever kill Billy Summers. Although, given a chance, he would certainly kill whoever else did it.'

For someone who could soon be facing a murder charge, Jimmy Beaton seemed strangely unmoved. Neither did he appear too surprised to see me.

'Hullo, Al,' he greeted. He then looked me up and down. 'I thought you might be here sooner or later. Sorry about the training,' he chuckled. 'Have you come down to take me and Micky Barnes for a few exercises? You can tell that old geezer in there that we wouldn't mind going for a run.'

'What happened, Jim?' I asked curtly, refusing to be drawn into his false levity.

His smile vanished. 'I'm not saying, Al, not even to you.'

'Jim! That detective in there is talking about a murder charge and you and Micky Barnes are his first two suspects!'

'That's crap, Al, and he knows it. It's a big bluff! I would never kill Billy. He was my best mate, you know that.'

'Jimmy, I tell you he's not bluffing. He's got twenty suspects in these cells and among them is the bloke that did it. He don't care which one it is; after all, no one is going anywhere. He'll charge you just as easy as he'll charge anyone else. And how about Micky Barnes? How does he come into this?'

Jimmy sighed and shook his head. 'Micky put one on a geezer at the party. The geezer asked for it, though, he kept taking the piss out of Micky about being black.'

Now Micky Barnes at fifteen and a half was the youngest of my players and unquestionably the most talented footballer of his age I had ever seen. He had represented London schools at every level and was due to sign as apprentice professional with Chelsea when he left school a few months later.

'Look, Jim,' I offered. 'If I can't say anything in your

favour then I'll say nothing, but just tell me what happened, eh?'

He thought for a moment, then said, 'Have a word with Micky, then, and if he agrees . . .' he nodded a quiet assent.

I spent the next fifteen minutes travelling backwards and forwards between the two cells and the detective inspector's office. At first I thought Micky was as reticent as Jimmy had been, but then I discovered he had been drinking heavily at the party and remembered very little.

'I was on the old Southern Comfort, Al,' he told me. 'It's bleedin' magic stuff.'

Slowly a picture emerged. It appeared that Billy and Jimmy had had one of their regular disagreements soon after arriving at the party. An argument had followed but subsequently died down. Micky, doubtless because of his tender years, had not been taking his Southern Comfort too graciously. He was eventually 'spoken' to by a number of youths from east London who were also at the party. One of this group was rash enough to pass some derogatory remark about Micky's colour. Micky then threw a pretty ferocious punch and his tormentor was knocked straight through a window. Being outnumbered by some twelve to three, my trio were at a disadvantage. They were at an even greater disadvantage when someone buried a knife in Billy.

A party fight between rival groups is confusing at the best of times, but when someone lies dead it is chaos. The first fact to emerge in the police enquiries was that Jimmy and Billy had had a ferocious, if short, argument a few minutes before the stabbing. The second was that it was Micky who had struck the first blow. In such circumstances, it is a great temptation for any investigating officer not to look much further for his case. I pointed out to the pair of them that now might be a very good time to tell the DI exactly what happened. They both agreed.

There was little more that I could achieve at the police station so I said my goodbyes and returned to the park.

There I was surrounded by curious players all eager to know the latest details.

'This is really serious, you know,' muttered Tony Randall the team captain, and now quite genuinely worried. 'That pair in there are our top scorers.'

I thought it was a particularly tasteless remark to have made but I did share his sentiments.

Late the following afternoon, Jimmy Beaton phoned to thank me and say that he had been released with no charges against him. Micky Barnes, on the other hand, was to be charged with causing an affray. On balance, this was not a bad result. Micky had, after all, struck the very first blow; he was therefore certain to be charged with something. His obvious defence would be to plead self-defence, or even justification. Considering there were two or three manslaughter charges scattered around the east London gang, my two had done quite well. The same, alas, could not be said for poor Billy.

It was to be four months before the case was heard at the Old Bailey. I placed a written request via my superintendent to Scotland Yard for permission to attend on the day and speak on behalf of Micky Barnes. To my surprise the request was readily granted. It was never my wish to defend Micky for becoming drunk and starting a fight that caused the death of his friend. That was something he would have to live with. What concerned me, however, was the punishment he might receive. Although I knew Micky had great *talent*, I also knew he did not have great *application*. If he was to spend very long 'inside' then his natural gift would simply disappear. He would never have either the determination or application to pick himself up after a year or two away from the game. With encouragement, I honestly believed Micky could go right to the very top. I was determined to try and give this encouragement.

On the day of the hearing Micky pleaded guilty and his counsel asked the judge if I could be allowed as a character witness. His Lordship agreed and the rare sight of a uniformed police officer standing on the other side of the fence at the Old Bailey aroused no little comment. I pointed out that within a few weeks Micky was due to begin a new career. I said that he had incredible talent and was quite the best I had ever seen. If he was put away it would be a tragic waste. His Lordship was sympathetic and gave Micky a deferred sentence. This meant that he must return to the court six months hence and, provided he had committed no further offences, he could be released without more ado.

'On the basis of what you say, officer, I shall watch his career with great interest,' commented His Lordship.

I did not wait for the manslaughter sentences, although they were mostly of two-year duration. It was now at the end of the football season and other than a phone call of thanks from Micky, I neither saw nor heard of him for some months. When next I saw him he had just emerged from a betting shop. I called and asked how he was progressing in his new career as an apprentice football professional.

'I'm not, Al, I didn't sign for Chelsea after all.'

'But why ever not?'

'Didn't fancy it, Al. I got bored with all that training.'

'What're you doing for a living, then?'

'I work in a butter ware'ouse, Al. Ain't a bad job really.'

'But how about your football? Aren't you interested in becoming a professional?'

'I did 'ave a trial for Arsenal, Al.'

'And?'

'Nuffink! They didn't pick me out, Al.'

I found that unbelievable. To see Micky just move down a touchline should have brought joy to the heart of any football scout.

'Did you score?' I asked hopefully.

'Nah, Al, I didn't get a chance. I played centre-half.'

'Centre-half! But why? You've never played centre-half in your life?'

'Yeh, I know I ain't, Al, but I just fancied playin' there.

133

I told 'em that it was me usual position.'

I could have wept.

'So what now, Micky? Have you given the game up?'

He shrugged. 'Well, it's true I ain't played a lot lately but I did git a letter from West 'Am. They said if I can tell 'em when I'm next playin' they'll come an' 'ave me watched.'

'Have you been training?'

'No, Al.'

'Look, come training with us. I'll give you three games to get fit and then I'll write to West Ham for you and tell them where you'll be playing. How does that suit you?'

'Fanks, Al, fanks a lot! That'll be smashin'.'

Needless to say, Micky did not come training with us, neither did he turn up for our match the following Saturday. Neither of course did I write to West Ham. The betting shop was far too great a draw for Micky, nothing could compete with that.

The last time I heard of Micky he had actually stopped losing money in these shops. He had got himself a gun and taken to holding them up instead. The only trouble was, there was hardly a betting shop in south-east London that did not know him. When they caught him, he went once more to the Bailey. This time there was no deferred sentence and no one spoke up for him. His five-year stretch may not have cured Micky of his mania for betting shops but it cured me of picking out football stars of fifteen!

12. There's always a way out

It had been quite a day. The station football team was top of the league, Jimmy Greaves had been transferred back from Italy to Tottenham Hotspur, and Joan had presented me with an 8lb 12oz daughter. After a cursory check to make sure her bits were all working, we then had to find a name. What a problem that turned out to be. How parents manage who have a dozen kids I will never know. We finally settled on Christine, after the tennis player Christine Truman. In actual fact tennis bores me to tears but we had both admired Miss Truman's spirit. (In addition I fancied her like mad.) Perhaps my parenthood gave me a new maturity, or at least my superintendent hoped it would, for the following day he recommended me for the advanced driving course. It began to seem that I was always on courses.

I had been driving the station general-purpose car and 'hurry-up' van on and off for a couple of years, but this latest offer meant I would spend five weeks at the Hendon Driving School and then be allowed to drive the big three-litre Wolseleys, Jaguars, Humbers and Rovers – the sole proud prerogative of the advanced driver. I leapt at the chance, and early one crisp December morning a month or so later I reported to the driving school.

One cannot undergo an advanced driving course without travelling at some very high speeds. I had always been a somewhat nervous passenger and with three students and an instructor to each car, it meant that my right foot spent hours each day in phantom braking. Sometimes, as the needle crept close to the 100 mph mark, I would slip slowly from the back seat and almost to the floor. The difference between driving at the more moderate speeds and those required for the course is enormous. It is not until a driver attempts these speeds that the flaws begin to show.

For me the most impressive instructors in a particularly impressive team, were the two who alternated on the 'skid-pan'. This pan is an area of smooth macadam that is daily soaked in oil and water. Paths and criss-cross lanes are marked out across the pan with old white-walled rubber tyres. Into these lanes two cars are driven, both with treadless and overinflated tyres.

During these five weeks, a student receives several hours of instruction in this particular skill and on the last week of the course he undergoes the 'skid-pan chase'. The 'bandit' moves off on to the pan with the student poised in another car a few yards behind. The two heavy old Wolseleys that were used for this work required a great deal of steering, and within seconds the sweat pours as the car is thrown into the sharp-turning lanes.

After five minutes the student is like a limp rag and convinced it is impossible to go any faster on the surface without the vehicle turning over. The bandit, on the other hand, calmly steers with one fist while holding his pipe with the other. It really is the most demoralizing experience. Most students, though, really enjoy the course and find it is over all too quickly.

Having attained the advanced status, a driver is obviously extremely reluctant to relinquish it. The slightest dent or scratch will prompt the garage sergeant to suspend the driver immediately. As a result, drivers go to incredible lengths in offering the most ingenious of excuses. As a radio-operator, I had worked on the area-car for some two years and I was lucky to have served an apprenticeship with a driver who, for me, was the king of them all.

Ron Hunt was easily the best driver I have ever ridden with. No matter the speed, I always had total confidence in his ability. Through red lights; the wrong side of traffic lanes; across pavements, up kerbs and down alleys. Ron could, and did, take a car anywhere at any speed. He was superb as a driver and just slightly better as a liar. This was always to serve him well but never better than in an incident that now lives in police-driving folklore.

One cold, wet November night, a few weeks before my Hendon course, I walked my Old Kent Road patrol and met my friend Doug Sorrell, who was on the neighbouring beat. As we sheltered in a deep doorway, the area-car prowled slowly near. We gave a wave of acknowledgement and Ron braked to a halt.

Winding down the window he called across the pavement, 'Do you two layabouts want a ride?'

Needing no further encouragement, we were across the pavement and into the car before he changed his mind. Carrying unauthorized passengers was a discipline offence and few drivers would risk it. Ron, on the other hand, was never a great one for the rules and there was usually at least one grateful foot-duty copper secreted low down in the warm on the back seat. That night there were to be two.

The force had far fewer vehicles in those days and most area-cars covered at least two police manors. In our case, we shared with Clapham police on an alternate-month basis – a particularly ridiculous set-up, because at least five police stations were very much closer. This dual coverage presented one great problem. There was the obvious one of not knowing the other station's manor, but the main drawback was Ron's total abhorrence of the whole Clapham area. He could not stand it. Other than two quick obligatory drives around the perimeter each tour of duty, he would never go anywhere near it, unless of course he received an emergency call.

The only other occupant of the car that night was the radio-operator and ex-Palestine policeman, Clive Banbury. Clive was an enthusiast who each day experienced at least one earth-shattering idea which he considered the whole world should try. As Doug and I slid into the back seat, Clive seemed to take some delight in reminding Ron he had yet to perform the first of his Clapham sprints. Ron would usually accomplish this dash once around midnight and again around 3 a.m. Muttering under his breath, Ron rammed the lever into first gear and we roared away with bow-waves of water spilling on to the pavement.

The route to Clapham was usually unvaried. Ron would throw the car irritably into the Vauxhall one-way system and speed straight through to Battersea Park, a mile or so further on. This one-way system is particularly complex, with six main roads converging. Above the system run some eight mainline railway tracks funnelling their way to Waterloo. As we turned sharp right under the first of the bridges, Ron released a quick 'Sod it'. The cause of this oath was a huge mobile trestle that blocked out most of the street light and reached up to the underside of the bridge. Maintenance staff who were cleaning and painting looked down in some apprehension at the screeching Wolseley.

We swerved hastily around the obstruction and within the next few minutes had completed the first of Ron's two reluctant nightly circuits. The rain had gained even more momentum and seemed to have driven everyone else from the streets. Clapham – or what little we saw of it – was as bare as a plague-city.

It was around 3 a.m. most night-duties that I usually became hungry. It was at that time that both Doug and I hinted to Ron that a hot pie from the coffee stall at Chelsea Bridge would not come amiss.

'You could get your second sprint around Clapham finished at the same time,' I suggested.

'We'll buy you a pie,' Doug bribed.

The offer was enough. Ron did not simply have a good appetite, he was a gannet. Two minutes later we raced towards Vauxhall. We were about to turn the corner under the first bridge when Clive thoughtfully reminded Ron of the badly lit scaffold. Grunting a mumbled thanks, he indicated that he had indeed forgotten the previous incident. To allow for the half of the road that was closed, Ron took a different line of approach into the corner. This he was able to do with ease since, because of the rain, we appeared to be the only vehicle still on the road. We slewed into the turn and, sure enough, there was the scaffold. The only problem was that it was now on the opposite side of the road! Our fears were as nothing to the three workmen's at the top of that trellis. Even in the dark I could see the terror on their faces! Every other driver I have ever travelled with, including myself, would have carried scaffold, workmen and probably us, into the nearby Thames before their foot had touched the brake. On the other hand, no other driver that I have ever met would have found himself in such a daft situation in the first place. The car jerked, swerved and finally accelerated, missing the first of the tubular poles by a hair's breadth.

This action was to lead us to stage two of the situation, i.e. Clive's criticism. Now excellent driver though he was, Ron was also somewhat sensitive, even downright touchy. It was rather unfortunate that he could not take criticism, because in criticism Clive was an absolute master. For the next mile it was explained to Ron in great detail just how he went wrong. Doug and I said nothing as Ron's resentment ticked away like a timebomb.

Finally we reached the south end of Chelsea Bridge Road. The coffee stall was just a minute away. At the foot of this road is a small, tight roundabout surrounded by a low brick wall. Considering our speed and the weather conditions, I thought Ron drove through this obstacle rather well. Clive, however, had the bit between his teeth and was letting nothing pass.

'Now take your approach to that last hazard, for example,' he went on. 'There's no doubt at all in my mind that you lined up wrong. It's all a question of centrifugal force, you know. Now if you had –'

Ron smashed the brake pedal to the floor, we each jack-knifed forward in unison.

'Right!' he bellowed. 'I've just about had enough of you!'

With that he did a swift three-point turn and retraced our route some sixty yards back from the roundabout approach. At this stage I thought he was going to repeat the circuit to silence the carping Clive.

'Here you are,' he snapped, pointing to the wheel and sliding out of the driving seat. 'You do it, clever dick. You just show us how it should be done. And I'll tell you what!' His eyes narrowed as he wagged a thick finger into Clive's face. 'You had just better get it bloody right!'

Doug and I looked at each other in horror. It was true that Clive could drive, but he was not a classified police driver by any means. We now found ourselves as unauthorized passengers, in a car driven by an unauthorized driver, four miles off our beat on another police manor, while shopping for a hot meat pie. I could think of at least a dozen discipline offences with no effort at all. We would not just get the sack, we'd probably get transported for life.

Eagerly Clive slid behind the wheel, while Ron walked angrily around to the front passenger door and slammed it shut behind him. Clive then adjusted his driving seat by rocketing it back on its runners straight into poor Doug's ankles. The new driver then realigned his mirror, cleared his throat and put the car into gear – reverse gear!

'Where the hell are you going?' demanded Ron, glaring at him.

'It's all right, it's all right,' soothed Clive. 'I just want to get a good run at it.'

That was the final straw for me. Rain or no rain, I would sooner be plodding the Old Kent Road in head-high floods than be a part of Clive's theory on the speedy negotiation of roundabouts.

'Let's get out,' I whispered anxiously to Doug.

This request, however, was as impractical as everything else that night. First, we were four miles off our manor in a monsoon without even a coat. We had both left them back at the station to dry out. Secondly, we were at least out of sight in the back of the car. We had no choice, all we could do was to cross fingers and pray.

The reversing ceased and there was a second's pause. Suddenly there was a crash of the gear-box and we began to approach the roundabout with an enormous roar. I assessed our speed at about 20 mph too fast. We needed to complete three-quarters of the circuit before we turned off towards the bridge. To my utter surprise we almost managed half of it before disaster struck. This 'centrifugal force' that Clive had so bewildered us with obviously decided to come in on the action. The rear of the car suddenly swung wide and the front off-side crashed against the brick wall, throwing us away at a sharp left angle. The bewildered Clive then snatched at the gear lever and for the second time in as many minutes managed to alarm us with his choice of reverse! The car promptly hurtled back and struck the wall once again, this time on the *rear* off-side wing. We sat in a silent thirty-second eternity as the overburdened wipers threw water off in all directions.

'Switch off!' screamed Ron.

Clive, for the first time in his life, almost admitted a mistake.

'I think I was a mite fast there,' he said confidentially.

'A mite f –' began Ron but he choked on his words.

He had never had an accident in his entire police service (well, at least not a *reported* one) and now an absolute cruncher was going to be put down to him – and him not even driving! Once Ron was able to string a sentence together, I thought he showed remarkable calm. 'Right, let's think about this. There has to be a way out somehow. There always is.'

I for one could not share his optimism. To me it looked a classic opportunity for some blind panic.

'First,' continued Ron, 'we've got to do something about you two. You'll have to get yourselves a cab or something back to the Old Kent Road. Then,' he cast a weary glance at the unusually subdued Clive, 'I've got to do something about you.'

'I would have thought the car should be highest on your list of priorities,' suggested Doug.

'It is, it is,' snapped Ron irritably. 'But I must get rid of you two first. Now quick, hop it.'

'But we haven't got coats,' I complained.

'Coats? Coats? I don't care if you are stark-bollock naked! Will you just sod off from here?'

Taking the hint, Doug and I turned up our jacket collars and emerged into the late-November rain. 'Get a cab,' Ron had ordered. Well, there were two problems with that suggestion. Firstly, Doug and I had about two shillings between us, and secondly, neither of us was particularly cab-orientated. I might, for instance, have considered a taxi if I had but two hours to live, but the worry of watching that meter always outweighed the convenience of any cab. No, we would walk.

The location of the accident – if Clive's little adventure could be termed an accident – was bleak to say the least. The area was a huge mass of railway-sidings, gas-works and old stone-yards. In fact between that roundabout and the scaffolders at Vauxhall, a distance of one mile, the only house on the route was the Battersea Dogs' Home.

Doug and I offered Ron our final 'Are-you-sure-we-can't-help?' gesture and then we left the scene. Before we turned out of sight, I shot a last glance over my shoulder. Ron had the buckled boot-lid raised and was rummaging around inside. Of Clive there was no sign. The rain continued unabated.

To avoid the risk of discovery by any supervising officer, Doug and I took a complicated and devious route through alleys, flats, courtyards and climbed the fence of a closed park. The problem with this route was that it put another fifty minutes on a journey that was already too long.

'It'll be our luck to find the Old Kent Road's burnt down in our absence,' I complained.

'It's more likely to be awash,' responded Doug, raising his eyes to the dark wet heavens.

The rain no longer bothered us; one can only become so wet. Eventually, some ninety minutes after the accident, we reached the back gate of our station. We needed to tip-toe to the boiler room where, ironically, we had left our coats to dry. Doug rang the switchboard on the internal telephone and was assured by George Pearsall that no one had missed us. We were somewhat surprised at this but then it had been such a dog's night that the duty officer had not ventured out of the station. Instead he had used the opportunity to catch up with his mounting paperwork. Removing our shirts and wringing out our socks, we laid them on the old coke boiler. They would never really dry there, of course, but at least we would experience the luxury of a sort of 'warm-damp'.

Two minutes to six, with sodden underclothes and bone-dry raincoats, we made our way to the sergeants' locker room where each shift was dismissed at the end of its tour.

'Have you heard the news?' our excited colleagues asked. 'Ron Hunt and Clive Banbury were killed a couple of hours ago in a crash in the area-car over on Clapham's manor!'

Police stations are worse than prisons for rumours.

'If Clive *is* dead then I've a bloody good idea who killed him,' chuckled Doug.

'No jury would convict him, though,' I responded. 'Not after having "a good run at it", they wouldn't.'

At first the rest of the shift were puzzled by our levity but we hinted, no more than that, that the demise of the area-car crew was an exaggerated tale to say the least.

A few minutes later Sergeant Ford entered the room to book us all off-duty.

'Are we all here?' he asked, glancing around the room and mentally totalling the numbers. 'Any reports?'

'No, sarge,' he was assured. 'It's so wet out there that there's only stupid coppers walking the streets.'

'Oh yeh? Well, some of 'em don't look too wet to me. Look at you two for a start.' He nodded to Doug and me. 'I bet you've spent half the bloody night in shop doorways.'

'Sarge, that's libellous!' complained Doug. 'I bet we've walked further tonight than anyone else at this nick.'

I was a little worried at Doug's bravado. We were by no means out of the woods yet.

'Okay, off you go, straight home and sleep tight,' bade the sergeant.

Although beat-duty coppers finished their night-duty at 6 a.m., the area-car overlapped them until 7 a.m. It says a great deal for our sense of concern that Doug and I decided to wait for Ron and Clive.

At ten minutes to the hour, the heavy throb of diesel disturbed us from our slumped position in the canteen chairs. We hastened into the yard in time to see a low-loader conveying the battered area-car through the back gates. The half-light of dawn had revealed the full extent of Clive's handiwork. It was not good. Ron sat tight-lipped alongside the driver while Clive gave us both a cheery wave.

'How'd you make out with the garage sergeant?' we asked anxiously.

Ron nodded secretively towards the canteen and the four of us entered in silence, while the low-loader manoeuvred across the station yard.

'We may just have got away with it,' Ron said hopefully.

'I don't believe it!' I exclaimed. 'A whack like that? No chance.'

'Shss!' he hissed. 'The garage sergeant knows the story is a load of old cobblers but he can't prove it. That's all that matters really.'

'Whatever did you tell him?'

'Blow-out! We had a blow-out to the front off-side tyre. Explains everything, don't it?'

'What d'you mean, "blow-out"? That's ludicrous. You can't have a blow-out just like that! Besides, he would only have to look at the tyre to see that wasn't on.'

'But we *gave* it a blow-out. Well, at least, I did.' He glanced darkly at Clive. 'He wasn't a lot of help, though.'

'But how did you blow-out the tyre, and how did you explain all the damage to the car?'

'Well, I said we were travelling at a normal speed around the roundabout when there was a loud bang and the front off-side wing pulled straight into the low brick wall. The car then ricocheted from the wall and slewed around causing the rear off-side corner also to strike the wall. Taking a normal line through the roundabout the off-side wheels would only be a foot or so from the wall anyway, so it's quite plausible and could easily happen.'

'Plausible! It's about as plausible as a flying pig. He never believed that yarn for a moment, surely?'

'I *told* you he didn't believe it! The point is that he can't prove otherwise, can he?'

'But how on earth did you fake a blow-out?' asked Doug.

Ron glanced quickly around the canteen before replying. 'With this.'

He slipped from his inside pocket an evil-looking stiletto. I recognized it at once. We had stopped a West Indian some weeks before, concerning possession of some property. We had taken him back to his home to confirm his address, and an hour or so later I had noticed the stiletto nestling between the back seats. There was nothing we could do about it at that stage, so we had decided to keep it in the car's tool-box. 'Never know, might come in handy,' Ron had prophetically remarked.

'But how did you manage to stick it into the tyre?' I asked.

'Not easily, it took me bloody ages. I got absolutely soaked. Him –' he nodded to Clive. 'He just sat in the car taking R/T messages. "We must keep a listening watch," he kept saying. He bloody nigh writes off the car and kills us all, then sits in the warm while I get pneumonia!'

'So what was the garage sergeant's final verdict?'

'He said I was a bloody liar.'

'Well, we all know that,' retorted Doug. 'But are you suspended or not?'

'Yes, but only temporarily while they investigate the circumstances. I should hear one way or the other by the end of the week.'

'Did the garage sergeant say anything to you, Clive?' I asked with mild curiosity. I was instantly aware I had said the wrong thing.

Clive raised his eyes in resignation to the now drying heavens. 'Oh, you *would* have to open your big mouth, wouldn't you?' He nodded in Ron's direction. 'He'd almost forgot – but now you've reminded him.'

'Well I'm sorry, I'm sure, but I was only curious as to what the garage sergeant said.'

'I'll tell you what the bloody garage sergeant said!' fumed Ron. 'He said, "Did you see any part of this accident, PC Banbury?" And do you know what PC bloody Banbury said?'

I had to admit I did not.

'Well, PC bloody Banbury who, I might add, had just managed to collide with a brick wall on a stationary roundabout, at three in the morning with no bugger for miles, said, "Oh no, sergeant, I didn't see a thing. I was busy on the set taking messages." That's what bloody Banbury said!'

Later that week, after an enquiry, the verdict came through: 'Accident not to count against the driver, damage caused by vehicle defect. Driver to be immediately reinstated.'

The garage sergeant's disbelief in Ron's story was exemplified by the offending tyre being sent first to Hendon then subsequently back to the manufacturers.

The combined verdict was that it was unarguably a blow-out, but still the question remained, how?

Ron left us a few months later. He transferred to C8 department at Scotland Yard (The Sweeney) where his imaginative talents were no doubt used to even greater advantage. Although I sadly missed him, the lessons he taught remained with me for the remainder of my police career. When I was eventually called upon to use them, not only did I avoid a six-month suspension, but also the wrath of one Sergeant Wilkin ('Mac') McCorkendale, a paranoid Aberdonian and the tightest man south of the Clyde.

It was Mac's old bike that was the cause of the trouble, that is if one can forget my own slight lapse while driving. This cycle was his pride and joy and had been so ever since he had bought it secondhand when he left school in 1928. It was a huge, black-painted, twin-crossbarred monster that contained more iron than the average tank. Well-meaning colleagues had from time to time asked him why he did not change it. It was apparently the devil's own job to pedal.

'I've nae money to fritter away,' Mac would answer. 'Yon cycle cost me seventeen shillings an' sixpence. That was an awful lot o' money in those days.'

The station cycle-rack was under a railway arch in the far corner of our yard. It was because of this very location that Mac refused to use it. 'Anyone can take it from there,' he would point out. 'I like to keep it where I can keep a good eye on it.' There was an element of truth in this. There were many non-cyclists at the station who would only too easily borrow a bike from the communal rack. Mac therefore always kept his at the foot of the steps that led up from the yard to the front office.

I had just taken over the night-duty area-car and was about to examine the vehicle – an essential precaution, because once I had signed for it any damage would be down to me. 'Whispering Taff' Reece, my quietly spoken R/T operator had, however, just taken our first call. A PC had two suspects under observation at the rear of some shops and he needed some help. Postponing my check, I leapt into the car. I found myself somewhat boxed in, first by the station van and secondly by a maintenance truck owned by the firm who were relaying the surface of our yard. Cursing at this annoying waste of time, I shunted backwards and forwards before roaring out into the street. I was certainly aware that Taff muttered *something*, but as ninety per cent of everything he said was totally inaudible, I had paid scant attention.

Forty-five minutes later I swung back through our gates with the PC and his two shop-breakers on board. Again there was a muttering from Taff. This time I requested a repeat.

He leaned over confidentially. 'All I said was, "Will you be running over Mac's bike again?"'

I braked to a head-rocking halt. 'What d'you mean, "again"?'

'Well, you drove over it three times on the way out. I just wondered if you fancied doing it once more for luck on the way back.'

The instant he spoke I knew exactly what had happened. The vehicle had certainly bumped up and down with each shunt that I made, but I had simply put it down to the disturbed surface of the yard.

I could hardly bring myself to look at the bike. The car had not so much damaged it as eaten it. While the prisoners were escorted into the charge room, I made a quick examination of the car. There were two deep scratches along the whole nearside. Neither Taff nor I had actually heard them being made and it could possibly have been down to the late-turn driver. On the other hand the scratches were consistent with the demolition of a cycle. In any case I had now been in possession of the vehicle for three-quarters of an hour and it was a bit late to put the damage down to someone else.

'There is always a way out,' Ron had said. He was

right but it was a long time coming.

Before we did anything at all, we needed to discover the whereabouts of Sergeant Wilkin McCorkendale. We were in luck! He was station officer for the night *and* he was at court next morning at ten o'clock. This meant he would not look at his bike for another nine or ten hours.

Less than four hundred yards from the station was a Ministry of Works garage where a twenty-four-hour maintenance staff worked on the Ministry vehicles. Frank Butler, the foreman, was an extremely cooperative fellow and could be my salvation.

He looked at the scratches thoughtfully. 'Well, it's black and we've got plenty of black paint. It'll need more than one spray, though. Wash it over and we'll see how it goes.'

During the next six hours Frank did three sprays down the side of that car. In between times I raced it around the manor drying it out and accepting calls. Taff asked if we should have had a 'wet paint' sign on the vehicle. My main fear was that it would rain or, even worse, become windy. I had visions of returning the car at 7 a.m. in fish-and-chip papers and bus tickets.

A little after 1 a.m. we had smuggled Mac's cycle into the Ministry garage.

'Nothing I can do about that,' said Frank shaking his head sadly.

'I know it can't be *mended*, Frank,' I agreed. 'But can you just straighten it out so it looks all right from a distance?'

'Oh, I can do that all right. I'll shove some of that black paint on as well. Not much I can do about the spokes, though.' He wrenched away a few of the more badly broken ones. 'It looks more like a busted brolly than a bike.'

I do not know how much Ministry work Frank accomplished that night. If he was not spraying the police car, he was hammering McCorkendale's cycle. What I do know is that he did a masterly job.

'Bit soft, I'm afraid, Ginger,' he murmured as he smoothed his hand along the bottom of the car doors. 'But not bad under the circumstances, I suppose.'

I parked the now gleaming area-car in its bay just before 7 a.m. I pointed out to the early-turn driver the perils of leaning anywhere on the nearside for a couple of hours. Mac's cycle had been returned to its customary position shortly before dawn and from a distance of ten yards looked no different. I did feel a little guilty about that, but an accident in a station yard was just about the most heinous crime in the garage sergeant's calendar. He would show more tolerance of a three-car pile-up than clouting the station officer's bike.

I had a troubled sleep that day. I kept thinking about what Mac would say, first when he returned from court and then when we all reported back for night-duty. To my amazement he said nothing, neither that night nor any other night. All he did was to wander around the yard with a torch examining the bottoms of the dozen or so vehicles parked there.

'You're too late, sunshine,' whispered the watchful Taff, almost to himself. 'A whole bloody twenty-four hours too late.'

The rest of the relief began to wonder why Mac had taken to using the cycle-rack instead of the usual position at the foot of the staircase. Taff and I did not enlighten them. I would sooner have dealt with the garage sergeant or even the Commissioner himself than a wronged Wilkin McCorkendale.

'Mum's the word, boyo,' whispered Taff.

He was dead right, of course. There had been a 'way out' after all, but we still needed to be discreet. Ron would have liked that.

13. Vinegar, perfume and John Donne

Southwark is one of London's most resilient boroughs, with a history that stretches back to the Romans via Dickens and Shakespeare. It has survived plague, pestilence and Hitler. In spite of these natural and manmade disasters, the closest call the old borough ever had was in the early 1960s. Those narrow streets, alleys and lanes that had miraculously survived the Nazi bombs were suddenly devastated by what appeared to be a rogue meteorite. The heart was practically torn out of the borough by swarming hordes of demolition men and builders. It seemed that for years the architects and planners who had been so busy in other parts of London were just itching to get at Southwark. When they did, they hit it with the ferocity of Norsemen.

The trend of the period was to set up soulless new towns in the dormitory countryside, then to offer financial incentives for local factories to move out to them. These firms provided the life-blood of the borough and had done so for generations. As factory after factory moved, and with them many small two- and three-man workshops, slowly a huge section of the young-adult population drifted away, leaving behind the elderly and infirm and the new immigrants.

Huge new estates were the rage, and one particular monstrosity was planned to run for almost a mile, from the Elephant and Castle to north Peckham. Sidestreets were to vanish; walkways in the sky were the vogue. Pensioners and young toddlers found themselves marooned twenty storeys up in the sky. People no longer gossiped across

151

alleys and tenement windows. Unless they met in the lift, they would not even *see* their neighbour for weeks.

For some reason architects are obsessed by the idea that old folk love nothing better than the happy sound of children's laughter. In reality old people hate kids, often with excellent reason. Time after time in these new estates, children's facilities are placed close to the old people's flats. Take Clamp's Court for example. This is a small, intimate quadrangle of spacious, one-storey bedsits for the elderly. It has a suntrap garden liberally scattered with lawns, rosebeds and benches. Most residents would consider the place perfect for their needs. *But*, it is surrounded on four sides by a comprehensive school, a primary school, a youth club and spacious council bungalows that cater entirely for the large family. Roughly a thousand children each day walk, run, fight, shout, skate, urinate, abuse, vandalize and ignite. The residents barricade themselves in and do not even answer the door.

As for the walkways in the sky – well! The theory was that the tenants could wander Tarzan-like from one part of the estate to another and never have to descend to ground level. The problem was that these walkways were invariably constructed above other people's bedrooms, so a shift worker not only has feet wandering about all over his head but also skates, stilts and small-sided ball games. I was subsequently to have an early experience of these estates that was not just a disaster, but damn near fatal. Perhaps I should have seen it as an omen for all of the years to come.

The euphoria of change in the sixties was so infectious that it eventually permeated down to the police force. It was to take at least ten years for us finally to emerge from the Neanderthal age but when the changes did come, they rumbled on with a slow but gathering momentum. The cloth ovens that served as ceremonial uniforms were thankfully withdrawn. Police-boxes (other than those in *Doctor Who*) disappeared. Then in 1961 some policemen were actually seen without jackets! This concession was fought tooth and nail by the traditionalists within the force. After all, if a copper was not wearing a jacket, where was he to wear the most nonsensical part of his entire equipment – the armlet?

The armlet, so we were told, made the difference between being a copper and not being one. It was only to be removed when we were off-duty. A whole lecture at the training school was devoted to the perils of entering licensed premises while off-duty and sporting an armlet! Of course, it was never explained what sort of burk would pop out for a quiet evening's drink wearing his helmet and full uniform. Yet in those traditionalists' eyes the two changes that infuriated them most were the abolition of the armlet and of the death penalty!

The loss of our armlets was not the only great reform, oh dear me no. The two others that instantly spring to mind were the switch to automatic gear-boxes on the larger police cars and the introduction of some new torches. How about that for an upheaval? At police driving school the cry was that automatic gear-boxes were for cissies. The whole theory of the police driving system was to be: 'in the right gear, in the right place, at the right speed'. Overnight the old drop-down-to-second-gear-and-away became a thing of the past. They did not like that at Hendon, not a bit they didn't. The reason for this sacrilegious change was purely financial. Someone had discovered that police drivers were going through more gear-boxes than traffic lights. An automatic gear-box in a police car had a life expectancy seven times that of its manual counterpart. There were to be no more dramatic chases in an engine-screaming second gear.

The second change – the new lamps – was about ninety years overdue. It had always seemed incredible to me that a force such as ours sent a man out in the dark with a lamp that would barely illuminate his wristwatch. Well, although the foot-duty coppers were still to keep their traditional corroded cauliflower torches, at least the area-cars were

153

given a new magic-beam. It was a handheld lighting unit that ran on a lead from a six-volt battery slung around the neck of the user. Its sharp, penetrating beam was good for a quarter mile.

A third, somewhat unofficial change, also took place at this time. Just for an experiment, a woman police constable was posted on the area-car for a week at selected stations throughout the force. For the Met police this was indeed quite a radical change. Up until the early seventies, girls rarely set foot on the streets. They stayed in the station and dealt mainly with women and children, both the victims and the prisoners.

At first, having a girl on the car was quite a novelty. Even members of the public raised an eyebrow or two. But we soon settled down and got on rather well. Ruth Bromley was a dark slim attractive girl with just the merest hint of a 'turn' in her eye. Strangely, this seemed to enhance her looks. That damp November Sunday was the last day of her week's experimental posting to the car. To be fair, nothing had been proved one way or the other. It had been an uncommonly quiet week and Taff Reece, my R/T operator, had hardly had to tear himself away from *Lady Chatterley's Lover* more than half a dozen times to take a call. The maddening thing about this inactivity was that, like Ruth, the new seek-and-search lamp had been on the car for a week and neither had been really tested.

Suddenly, just around dusk at 4.30 p.m. we received our first call of that late-turn duty. And what a call! It was absolutely made for our new lamp. I could not get the car to the scene quickly enough. 'Wyndham Road, SE5, twenty-storey block under construction. See informant, man attempting suicide from the top floor.'

Taff formally acknowledged the call. Then the operator at Scotland Yard's information room came back with an unusual and rare piece of advice.

'The informant seemed distressed about the situation. Handle him sensitively, will you?'

It is extremely rare for the information room to add anything to their original call. We immediately imagined that the informant must have been sobbing into the telephone or on the verge of a breakdown.

'Will do,' responded Taff gallantly.

The call had come from one of the first of the high-rise blocks to be built on our manor. There was a trio of them – still uncompleted, so as yet they did not have a name – on a vast site surrounded by a twenty-foot-high fence erected to keep out intruders. 'Intruders' it may have kept out, kids it didn't. Whenever the watchman crept away they would run riot.

Although we took only minutes to arrive, our arrival coincided with dusk, so we could not see details at the top of the building with the naked eye.

'Bunk me up over the fence an' I'll save 'im, sir. I will, I'll save 'im!'

I quickly turned to see who was responsible for this brave gesture, and was not in the least surprised to discover he was a scruffy swaying drunk.

'I told Scotland Yard, sir, I told 'em. "No man is an island," I said, sir.' I would dearly have loved to discover the cause of this poetic distraction but more urgent matters prevailed.

'Was it you that called the police?' I asked.

'Yessir! No man is an island, sir.'

'Which block is this man supposed to be on?'

'There's no supposed about it, s–'

'Look!' I cut in angrily. 'Just tell me where he is!'

'Follow me, sir, I'll show you, sir.' With that he inserted his left foot in the wire-mesh. He instantly slipped and fell forward against the fence.

I seized a rough hold of his jacket. 'Which block? Which bloody block is it?'

He pointed vaguely to the tower block at the far end. 'That one, sir, that one. No man is an island, though, sir; no man is an island.'

I could not switch on our lamp quick enough! Here was the perfect opportunity to test our new toy. With considerable difficulty I climbed to the top of the fence. Taff handed me up the lamp and I began to sweep the skyline dramatically. I soon picked out the towering block and began to trace its outline. Spotting a solitary swinging figure, I gave him full beam and illuminated him like some circus artiste. A roar of impressed approval came from our inebriate assistant. His interest now rekindled, he again tried to climb the fence but once more slipped and fell.

Keeping the beam fixed on the impending suicide victim, I tried to make out enough detail to form a plan of rescue. This was never going to be easy. The block was little more than a steel and concrete skeleton without walls, lift or staircase. Each floor was served by a builder's hoist but that could not be used because of the dangling figure. The obvious way seemed to be for the fire brigade to gain a slow access with their scaling ladders, one floor at a time.

I called down to Ruth to stay with the R/T set, firstly to call the brigade and an ambulance, and secondly to keep open an instant line of communication. Meanwhile Taff climbed the fence and ran across to the foot of the block in order to open some sort of dialogue with the marooned victim. I had eventually positioned myself, with a great deal of discomfort, astride the top of the fence, crossing my fingers that the battery would not give out until the brigade arrived.

After five minutes or so Taff reported breathlessly back. 'He's in a right state, boyo,' he panted, shaking his head. 'He just seems to be screaming. I think he's a nutter or a suicide whose bottle has gone. He's only just clinging on, though. If we don't get him down soon he's had it.'

I received this report with some smugness – it confirmed, after all, my own first impression.

'Can you hurry the brigade up, love?' I called down to Ruth with some urgency. 'And start taking a few particulars.' Then cupping my hands, I bellowed across the site, 'Hold on, mate, we'll soon have you down, don't worry.'

The distant sound of bells gave a comforting feeling as the first of the three engines swung into the far end of Wyndham Road. This was followed by an equally prompt appearance by the ambulance. So far, so good.

'What is your name?' I heard Ruth ask our drunken informant.

He was so intent watching me that he failed to hear her. Nor did he hear her when she repeated the question.

'Oy!' I yelled. 'Your name – give the girl a name.'

'Oh, sorry, sir, sorry.'

He turned around and staggered towards the car. Bending to the open window his face almost touched that of the young WPC. I saw her wince and she turned her head.

'Dunn, sir,' he muttered to her.

'What is your Christian name, Mr Dunn?' she asked.

'My name's not Dunn, sir.'

'But I thought – oh never mind. Just give me that name again.'

'Dunn, sir.'

She looked helplessly up at me.

'Is your bloody name Dunn or not?' I demanded. 'For Chrissake answer the girl.'

'My name is Ryan, sir.' He shook his head in frustration. 'Dunn is the bloke what wrote it.'

'Wrote what, Mr Ryan?' asked Ruth, now totally confused.

'"No man is an island", sir.'

It was bad enough trying to keep my balance on the fence, without being compelled to listen to this lunacy. I called irritably to the girl. 'Forget it. Just record that the informant was anonymous and left before our arrival. *And* get rid of that silly sod before the brigade turns up!'

Dutifully she slid from the seat and escorted Mr Dunn-

Ryan to the other side of the road and placed him in the now gathering crowd.

A white-helmeted fire officer left the first of the engines and ran to the bottom of my fence requesting a situation report. I explained the problem of access and together with three of his crew he slid a couple of scaling ladders from the storebox on the fire engine. They were over the fence within seconds and away into the darkness.

Retraining the beam on the crying man, I could see that he had now managed to obtain a foothold in addition to his handhold. It was only this factor that really prevented him from tumbling two hundred feet on to the site debris below. After some ten or twelve minutes of nail-biting tension, a great cheer from the watching crowd announced the arrival of the rescue team at the top of the hoist. With the aid of the ladder and a rope, the man was eventually pulled back into the comparative safety of the building. After a suitable time for recovery, he then joined the brigade in a descent. I was delighted to see this because it indicated that he was unharmed either physically or mentally. Keeping the beam on the party, I saw they were joined at the foot of the structure by Taff Reece and the younger of our two ambulance men.

All in all it had been a smooth, well-orchestrated operation between the emergency services, and our new lamp had already proved its worth. Several of the spectators said much the same thing. The next fact to be established was just what the intruder had been up to, or which of our local institutions he had escaped from.

I was quite surprised to see the rescue team and the rescued man walk towards a large padlocked gate in the fence. The man produced what seemed to be a key and locked the gate carefully after accompanying them through. The firemen in particular seemed highly amused. I put it down to their general good spirits after a grand job well done.

'Well, that's the finish, mate,' called out the white-helmeted fire chief, with the slightest of smirks. 'I've got all the details I need from this constable, but I think matey here wants a word with you. Cheerio!'

'Cheers,' I acknowledged.

'Oy! Are you the prat who started all this off?' was the intruder's surprise opening remark. I was taken aback. This was not the usual first approach of a suspect caught bang-to-rights. Neither was it the bewildered words of an indecisive suicide who had changed his mind.

'Well, I *coordinated* the incident, if that's what you mean,' I answered loftily. 'It's a good thing I did, too, otherwise you'd still be up there.'

'It's "up there" that I'm supposed to be! That's what I'm paid for! I'm a lift engineer and the hoist has broken. I was getting it ready for Monday morning when you lit me up like Brighton!'

'Well, why didn't you yell down and let us know you were okay?' I asked, now pleased that most of the crowd had gone. 'You caused everyone a great deal of trouble, you know,' I reproached.

'*I've* caused a great deal of trouble! *I* have?' he mimicked. 'How about you with that stupid torch? What have you caused, then, if it ain't been trouble, eh? I could have got down comfortably if I hadn't had that bloody great beam shining in me eyes. In any case, I was calling loud enough but your cloth-eared mate here assumed I was some bloody nutter!'

'Well, er, let's have a look at your credentials,' I requested, desperately seeking a way out.

He shook his head in mute frustration and thrust a grimy small card beneath my nose. It could have been anything; I could barely make out a word. I studied it knowingly for a moment. 'Yes, that appears to be in order,' I announced, attempting to preserve at least some dignity. 'You can go back now if you wish.'

'Oh no! No bloody fear! That's me done for the week-end. You've scared the shits out of me, you have, and I'm not going back there no more today. I'll tell them why, as well, when they ask me.'

I had no idea who 'they' were, but they did not sound as if they were going to be very pleased.

He walked towards a small battered van that rested on the opposite side of the road. I could still feel the embarrassment playing around my face and neck.

'Just a minute!' called Taff Reece, strolling across the road to the still fuming engineer. 'Is this your van?'

'Of course it is, why?'

'Well, your tax is out of date, two months to be precise.'

He looked at Taff open-mouthed. 'I don't believe it! This daft bastard does his best to kill me and now you're going to do me for no tax? What's the matter with you lot, have the police force declared war on me or something?'

'No, boyo, nothing like that. You're not going to be summonsed,' assured the Welshman. 'But in future, before you are rude to the sheriff, just make sure that he can't be even more rude to you.'

The engineer slammed his door angrily and drove away muttering to himself. I breathed a deep sigh of relief. 'I made a balls-up of that, Taff,' I confessed.

'Yes, you did, didn't you?' he needlessly agreed. 'Come on, I'll buy you a tea.'

This uncharacteristically generous offer was interrupted by squeals from the rear of the ambulance. Mr Dunn-Ryan had apparently decided he needed a pee. The ambulance men had rightly protested that the open door of their spotless vehicle was not a urinal. These protestations had drawn the attention of the fair Miss Bromley. Deciding that our informant had finally pushed his luck a shade too far, she told him she was arresting him for being 'drunk and indecent'. This was okay up to a point. What the enthusiastic Miss Bromley failed to do, however, was at least allow the unfortunate drunk the comfort of completing his pee. Having begun it on the back steps of the ambulance, he then completed it on the front pleats of her gaberdine skirt.

'I tell you now,' I said, 'I am not having him in my car.'

'But I've arrested him!' she objected.

'I know and I don't care. I'm not having any drunk in my car, especially one who was just pissed over everything. You will just have to wait for the van.'

'You'll have to wait a bloody long time, boyo,' reminded Taff. 'It's been out of service for three days.'

I groaned. 'Sod! I'd forgotten that. Okay, but he's your responsibility,' I pointed out. 'If he even remotely looks like being sick, then get his head out of that car window even if it's closed. There's nothing worse in a car than a drunk being sick.' Oh how wrong can one be! There is in fact something ten times worse than that, as we were to find out within minutes.

The prisoner had by this time become almost incoherent. He prattled incessantly about 'being an island', but few of his words made sense. I adjusted my driving mirror so I could easily see his face. I still had a gut feeling that he was about to be sick, and experience had taught me that even a second's delay can be disastrous. Ruth sat herself as far away from him as possible and dabbed at her skirt with a bunched-up handkerchief. Taff, on the other hand, seemed to find the whole scene mildly entertaining and asked the drunk for a song.

We were halfway to the station when the chat suddenly stopped. I glanced quickly into the mirror and saw that Dunn-Ryan had set his jaw in grim determination. For a second this puzzled me, but then a grunt and the sound of breaking wind made everything only too clear. I swung the car straight to the kerbside. 'Get him out! Quick, get him out!' Taff slipped out of the front door and had the rear door opened in almost one move. He grabbed the straining prisoner by the scruff of his neck and dumped him on to the pavement. Already the smell in the car was evil. Ruth cowered in the corner.

I examined the rear seat and was relieved to discover that

161

it could have been a great deal worse. There was the slightest of stains but most of the deposits were on the pavement, having seeped through the seat of his trousers.

'What can we do?' wailed Ruth. 'After all, I have arrested him.'

'That's the least of your worries!' I snapped. 'Mr Ryan!'

'Yes, sir?' answered the rapidly sobering prisoner.

'Mr Ryan, as from now you are de-arrested. Hop it.'

'But you can't do that,' protested the girl.

'But he *has* done it, lovely,' explained Taff.

For a moment we watched in fascination as the newly freed prisoner scuttled bow-legged down the Walworth Road.

'What *does* he look like?' I asked no one in particular.

'Well, unless they are close enough to smell him,' observed Taff, 'people are going to think he's either got badly chapped legs or he's doing John Wayne impressions.'

'Right, the car,' I reminded them. 'We've got to do something about that otherwise we'll never get rid of the smell.'

Ruth squeezed in with Taff on the front seat, much to his delight, and we were soon back in the station yard.

'We want a bucket, hot water and a mop, Ruth, and as many old rags as you can muster,' I instructed.

In the meantime I gingerly removed the entire back seat. We scrubbed and polished that old Wolseley until it shone, but it still smelt like a sewer.

'Vinegar!' exclaimed Ruth suddenly.

'What about it?' asked Taff and I almost in unison.

'I remember reading somewhere that it kills smells.'

'But vinegar itself can smell pretty awful,' I pointed out.

'Well, perhaps that is it. That could be how it works. Perhaps it neutralizes it or something.'

'Well, let's give it a try, then. Anything must be better than its present condition.'

Taff raced away to the canteen and soon emerged with a slender glass bottle. 'How do you put it on, boyo?'

'I dunno, I suppose you just shake it over everything like fish and chips.'

Taff gave the bottle a vigorous shake and Ruth smeared the droplets over the back seat with a handful of tissues.

'Look, it's nearly break time. Let's leave the seat in the boiler room. Perhaps it'll be okay by the time we've finished our tea,' I suggested hopefully.

The others agreed and Ruth then slipped away to change from her soiled civilian clothes into her uniform.

Forty-five minutes later, with the seat back in the car, we stood sniffing the air like a trio of bloodhounds.

'The only difference I can notice, boyo, is that it now stinks of both shit *and* vinegar.'

'Phew, Taff's right, Harry,' agreed Ruth. 'I think it's ten times worse.'

I nodded. 'I'll ring the district garage. Perhaps they have a spare R/T car secreted away somewhere.'

My quest was fruitless and a few minutes later I returned to the yard where my two colleagues stood poised by the opened doors of the car. Taff was shaking his head in some amusement while Ruth was now extremely close to tears.

'We've just found another antidote that doesn't work,' commented Taff. 'Stick your nose in there and give it a treat.'

There was no need to 'stick my nose in' at all. I could smell it four yards away.

'Good God! Whatever has happened now? It smells like a Bolivian brothel.'

'I'm sorry,' sobbed Ruth. 'I thought I would shake some perfume in there. You never know, it might have helped. But – well – the top came off!' she blurted.

It was the final straw. There was no more I could do to keep the car in service. Apart from the constabulary aspect, both Taff and I were married men. To arrive home around midnight reeking of Yardley is one thing. To explain it away by claiming that it was all caused by a drunk crapping in the car would strain the credibility of even the most tolerant wife.

On Monday I was summoned by the superintendent and asked how I thought the experiment had gone. Although Ruth never believed me, I said I was in favour of it. In spite of this recommendation, it was to be ten years before another female was posted to the area-car. However, ex-WPC Ruth Bromley, now a rotund mother of four, is still convinced that this decade of delay was due to an unfortunate combination of loose bottle tops and loose bowels. It would be a brave man who said she was wrong.

14. Kill the caretaker!

The years raced by alarmingly. Halfway through my service I found myself still policing the same area. I realized I was slipping deeper and deeper into the rut. I occasionally applied for posts in the more specialized departments, but already age was against me. This was never so apparent as on my interview and test as a physical training instructor with the police cadets. I was fine on the running, quite passable on the jumping, but my rope-climbing and boxwork were calamitous.

On one particular test the applicants were required to sprint the length of the gym and skim the box with little more than a fingertip touch. My approach indicated to everybody in the gym – sadly, except me – that I had more chance of going under the thing than over it. Eventually even I realized this, but not until I was less than two feet from it and running flat out. One of the fascinated watchers was an old cleaner who had seen most of the police gymnasts of the previous twenty years. He was reported to have said that until I actually collided with the box, he honestly thought I was going to fly over the damn thing. Later, with creaking and bloodied kneecaps, I attended my interview. I was asked by a rather benign chief inspector how well I thought I had done in the tests.

'Do you want the truth, sir?' I asked.

He shrugged. 'As close as you can get will do.'

'I though I was crap.'

'Well, we already have a classification written down here for you, but I think yours is marginally the more accurate. Anyway, thank you for attending, goodday.'

Because of this regular quest for other pastures, it had become apparent to the superintendent that I was suffering from the 'mid-service itch'. The novelty of the force had long worn off and I was becoming increasingly restless. By coincidence, around this time the home-beat system, or community coppering, had just been successfully tried in the suburbs and it was decided to extend it to the whole of the Metropolitan area. All that was lacking on our manor was the suitable candidate. Ideally it needed to be a man who was unlikely for promotion, somewhat devoid of ambition, in mid-service and approaching middle age.

'Cole,' said the superintendent. 'I have the very job for you.'

Once I discovered there was no night-duty involved I leapt at it, proving, of course, that one can take the right job for the wrong reasons.

The great difference between home-beating and policing as I had previously known it was its sheer informality. Many taboos that surrounded the force were broken down almost overnight. People who would never dream of talking to street-duty police would speak to the home-beat copper. I was to have an early experience of this. On at least three days each week I would call at a local baker's at lunchtime for a pie and a cream cake. The counter girls were particularly busy at this period and I would wander straight through the shop into their restroom. There I would prepare them each a cup of tea for when the main rush was over, usually around 1.30 p.m. Within a few days I sensed that Betty, a slim, attractive thirty-five-year-old, was anxious to talk. I made no obvious attempt to start a conversation, I simply made myself readily available should she feel so disposed.

Finally it came. 'Can I speak to you, Harry? Confidentially I mean – *really* confidentially.'

'Do you also mean unofficially?'

'Yes, that too.'

'Be my guest.'

The other girls, obviously sensing or even expecting some personal drama, gave us plenty of room as we huddled together over a small table.

'Do you know Matthew Skewse?' was her surprise opening remark.

'Yes, I know Matthew quite well. I taught him the manor when he first came to the station some ten months ago.'

'Oh,' she murmured, dropping her gaze. 'He's a friend of yours, then?'

'I didn't say that. You asked if I knew him and I told you I did. As a matter of fact I'm not all that keen on him, but I assume that has nothing to do with whatever's bothering you. Or has it?'

'It could have a great deal to do with it.' She paused and seemed to be searching for words.

'Look, Betty, I *know* Matthew Skewse, I don't *like* Matthew Skewse but that is not his fault. If you want to say something to me about Matthew in confidence then go ahead. But in fairness to you I must point out one thing. I have a gut feeling that you are about to say something really serious concerning him, yes?' She nodded. 'Very well, but Matthew *is* a serving copper and so am I. If it is something that I can remotely keep in confidence I will, but if what you say is going to turn out to be an allegation, I *may* well stop you and suggest you make it officially to a senior police officer. Okay, do you still want to tell me?'

She again nodded. 'I want to show you something,' she said, as she opened her handbag and took from it a thick brown envelope. 'My daughter Sharon has a Saturday job in a shoeshop down the market. While she was at work she got to know Skewse because he patrolled around there. If they were not too busy he would sometimes pop into the shop for a quick cigarette. I knew he was seeing her and I didn't like it one bit.'

'Did you say so?'

She sighed. 'No, Sharon is a big girl, although she's only fifteen. But I don't have a man behind me now that Alan has left me. If I was to upset her I'd have no one at all.'

'I can understand that.'

'Thanks. Well, I was sorting out the washing last week and I was about to pop Sharon's overall into the machine . . .' She paused and stared at me for some seconds. 'Well, I found this.' She bit her lip and toyed nervously with the small brown package, turning it over and over in her hands. 'Well, I've come this far, I suppose I'd better give them to you.'

Her voice had now thickened and I could see she was having great difficulty in keeping control. She slid the envelope across the formica-topped table and stared unblinking out into the shop proper.

I slipped open the flap and found, just as I had guessed, about a dozen or so photographs. They were each of a pretty, dark-haired, well-rounded young girl. Most of them were totally nude, but two or three contained just a wisp of underclothing. All had been posed on the same bed. Although sensuous, the pictures were by no means obscene. If anything, some were really quite tasteful.

'Have you spoken to her about them?'

'No, I just can't bring myself to. Oh, he took them all right, if that's what you're thinking. Sharon told me he had taken some pictures of her, she even showed me one or two. The ones she allowed me to see were either taken in my living-room or outside on the balcony. All the others . . .' her voice fell to a whisper . . . 'were taken on Sharon's bed.'

I cut in rather selfishly. 'I've got to tell you, Betty, you have put me in one hell of a spot. You've just made an extremely serious allegation about a workmate of mine. Tell me, what is it exactly that you want me to do?'

'What do I want you to do?' she echoed. 'I just want you to get him away from her, Harry, that's all. I want every picture of her that he's got and I want them burnt.' Her voice began to rise dramatically. 'And I never want him near my baby again, that's what I want!'

She gave a series of great sobs and the tears cascaded down her cheeks. I placed my arm around her shoulders and I felt them lift visibly at each of her great sobs.

'Betty, we've got to rethink the whole thing. It really is very serious for everyone concerned. Are you sure you still want this done unofficially?'

'I don't want any trouble that's going to involve my Sharon. I'll do anything to stop that. I have felt like sticking a knife in the bastard several times, but everyone would know about the pictures then, wouldn't they?'

'They certainly would,' I agreed. 'Look, I have just the glimmer of an idea. It probably won't work, but at least it's worth a try.'

'Try anything you like but they mustn't hurt my girl, she really is a good kid. I swear she is.'

'Betty, I've got to ask you to let me keep these pictures at least until tomorrow. Will you trust me with them?'

'Can't I burn her face out first with a cigarette or something?'

'I can't stop you from doing that – as far as I'm concerned they are your pictures – I'm just asking you not to, that's all.'

'All right,' she sniffed. 'Till tomorrow, then.' She glanced up at the wall-clock. 'Till about this time?'

'Till about this time, Betty.'

The whole situation would have been bad enough at the best of times, but it was made doubly difficult by our reigning superintendent. Not for nothing was he known as 'Nervous Norman'. As far as Nervous was concerned, a matter was either 'on paper' or it was not. There was no such word in his vocabulary as 'unofficial'. I needed someone in rank whom I could trust and, even more important, who would trust me. Rather unfairly I chose Inspector David Bryant. I say 'unfairly' because he had recently passed his selection board for the next rank. Just about the last thing a budding chief inspector needs is involvement in an unofficial action concerning a serving police officer and a nude female juvenile! If the story was to leak, it would be on half of the country's breakfast tables the following Sunday!

I made all haste back to the station and, unfortunately for Mr Bryant, found him alone in the inspector's office. It was too good an opportunity to miss. 'Er – I have this slight problem, guv' . . .' I began.

He listened to the story without interruption. When I had finished he uttered his first words. 'Just *why* is it, Harry Cole, that you don't want me to become a chief inspector?'

'I thought you might say that, guv',' I replied. 'Would you like me to see someone else less vulnerable?'

'No, sit down. First let's work out what we know about Skewse.'

Matthew Skewse was thirty-one years of age and had been a regular soldier. He joined the Metropolitan Police after serving seven years in the Scots Guards. He was very much a loner and suspiciously fond of the company of young, not overbright girls who would respond to almost anyone who showed them sufficient interest. Matthew had been divorced for some years and lived in the single men's section-house. He was still serving his probationary period and it was common knowledge that many of his relief were uneasy about his general character.

Bryant shook his head. 'I don't like this one bit. Are you absolutely sure the mother would not cooperate with anything *official*?'

'I'm certain.'

'Okay. Well, I'll need to see her. Do you think she would come here?'

'I would think so. I'll collect her if you like. She'll probably come easier with me.'

Thirty minutes later a tearful Betty sat between us and agonizingly recounted her story.

'You know, I'm not surprised,' he told me after Betty had left. 'There's something about that bloke that has had me wondering ever since he's been here. If we'd had someone with a bit of backbone upstairs this situation would have been resolved long ago. It's ridiculous that it has ever got to this stage.' He shook his head sadly. 'Skewse is weekly leave today, but he's on at six tomorrow. How about you, are you around tomorrow?'

I nodded. 'I'm on at two p.m.'

'Very well, come up and see me then. I'll know a little more by that time.'

The next day I climbed the two flights to the inspector's office with some trepidation. I was beginning to have second thoughts. After all, just because he was a loner was no reason for a witch-hunt. I wondered what my reaction would have been if he had been a personal friend instead of a shy introvert. The door was wide open and Inspector Bryant sat clattering away on a battered old typewriter. He looked down the corridor on my approach and beckoned me in.

'He's gone,' he said simply.

'What d'you mean "gone", guv'? Who's gone and where?'

'Skewse has gone – back to Dunfermline. After you left yesterday I changed my mind and decided to go to the section-house and see him as soon as possible. I looked in his room but he wasn't there. In direct contradiction to good sense and accepted procedure I had a nosey round. I found photographs of another half-dozen young girls. The maddening thing is they are all bloody good pictures. Some were really most beautifully posed. Anyway, I sent for him this morning. He made no attempt to lie, he simply put his hands up to everything. He even gave me another half-dozen snaps of your friend's daughter, and in four of them she's embracing another girl! He asked me if I was going to arrest him. I told him if it was down to me, he would be on the sheet for as many offences as I could think

171

of. When he realized that he wasn't going to be nicked he asked if he could resign and leave there and then. I rushed the paperwork through, made a couple of phone calls, and three hours later he was on the Perth train.'

'What happens now?' I asked.

'Nothing. Nothing at all, I hope. If it does, I'll never make chief inspector! Remember, Skewse has retired entirely of his own accord. He was quite entitled to do that. Your friend can have her daughter's pictures back – they are the only ones that are left now.'

'What happened to the other photographs?'

'I *suggested* to Skewse he may like to burn them in my presence. He agreed that was a very good idea.'

'Why didn't you burn young Sharon's as well?'

'Because her mother would never be really sure they had all gone. Incidentally, I think it may be as well not to mention anything to Sharon's mum about the photographs of Sharon with a partner. She's upset enough as it is.'

'I thought that all serving coppers had to work out a month's notice before they resigned, sir?'

'Ordinarily they do. However, we can make a "special provision". Skewse was a special provision.'

'Does Nervous – er, Mr Norman know about this, sir?'

'Nervous? Good God, no! He knows, of course, that Skewse has left us. Even Mr Norman wouldn't have missed that. No, he thinks it's a compassionate case. It wouldn't be a bad idea if he continues to think that. By the way, this case is not simply dead, you know, it has never even *existed*. Yeh?'

'Yeh,' I agreed.

'One last thing.'

'Sir?'

'I know you are required as a home-beat officer to develop a good relationship with your parishioners, but I do feel that making tea in the baker's is coming it a bit strong. D'you agree?'

'I agree.'

'Good lad.'

Other than the departure of Skewse, my introduction to home-beating was not really the success of the year. The crime rate did not alter, traffic was as bad as ever and the curate from Lorrimore Square Vicarage was still being tormented by kids. Whoever designed that vicarage must have been a class-one heretic. It was surrounded on three sides by large-family council flats with a youth club and nursery playschool immediately adjacent. I can only assume that the designer was taken with the Old Testament idea that the shepherd should be amongst his flock. If this was indeed the theory, then it was enormously successful. So successful that the kids adopted another Old Testament idea – stoning the vicar to death. Behind his shatterproof glass and chicken-wired windows, the tormented resentful priest fought a miniature holy war. Sad to say, God was not on the side of the angels. The devil's forces won hands down.

These missile-hurling juveniles were indeed a problem and I wondered how best to cope. One thing was sure, if I rushed around the parish stating, 'I'm your new police experiment – try me,' the only response I would get would be from nutters. Everyone else would clam up and avoid me like the plague. No, it had to be a completely different approach. I decided to settle for the slow-developing 'I'm-here-if-you-want-me' style. Of course, this approach is all very well in the long term, but in the short term it can need a little push. There was in fact quite an easy answer to that one – the children themselves. Perhaps I could do it through them in the schools? Apart from anything else, the children are often the only members of a family whom a copper sees with any regularity. Mum is frequently marooned some twenty storeys high and dad is usually at work all day. Only youngsters to-and-fro.

Well, at least I had a strategy, but I was not sure how to make the first approach. After much consideration I wandered into the local juvenile bureau, the police department that deals exclusively with children under the age of seventeen.

'Do you have any films?' I asked.

'What sort?'

'I dunno, perhaps something I can take into a school that might interest the kids. Preferably something that may stimulate a discussion, or even an argument.'

They offered me a collection of rather worn, blurred, jumpy shorts. Two of these films were certainly controversial, but for the wrong reasons. The first was an ancient one-reeler featuring the television presenter Valerie Singleton. She looked about twelve and was trying to cross a road in Kensington. The second was another road safety film and equally useless, shot on a sedate country road in Hampshire. 'Find a safe place to cross' and 'Never cross between parked cars' were the overriding themes, both utterly ridiculous. If children could not cross between parked cars on my patch they would never be able to cross a road at all. The borough streets are little more than one gigantic carpark. Children *had* to cross between them. What we needed, I decided, was a whole new road safety code.

I had a great piece of luck at this time: I met Ron Preston, a headmaster of a local primary school. All four of my schools had been enormously cooperative and we had developed a good relationship. Ron, however, was a home-movie buff and was always using his children in a local park. Ron, with his cast of thousands – well twenty, anyway – was looking for a new subject.

'Why don't we shoot our own road safety film?' he asked. 'We could set it in our local streets and the children would not only take part, but would associate themselves far more readily than in some contrived situation which in reality has nothing to do with them.'

I thought this was a superb idea. My only reservation was when he outlined the plot. 'We'll use Bert the school caretaker and we'll get him to cross the road without looking both ways. You can then come hammering down the street in your car and run him over.'

'Bit bloodthirsty, isn't it?' I winced.

'What is, killing Bert? No, not at all. You see,' explained Ron, 'whatever film we make, we have to kill the school caretaker. It's practically tradition, you know – the children expect it. This film will never have the necessary impact unless Bert rolls under your wheels. Don't worry,' he added sensing my doubts, 'Bert's quite used to it, he's had tons of experience. He's been shot to death with arrows, fallen on spikes from the school roof and riddled with bullets on numerous occasions. Being mangled by a car will be no problem at all for Bert – he'll enjoy it.'

'Don't the children like him, then?'

'Like him? They *love* him – they think the absolute world of him!'

'Well, is he – well, you know – a bit simple, perhaps?'

'Who, Bert, a bit simple? Good God, man, no! He's just a born ham. He simply adores acting.'

I was still unconvinced but Ron seemed so fired with his impending new masterpiece that I felt obliged to go along with him.

'Exactly how do you propose to do it?' I enquired, losing none of my doubts.

'Well, it'll probably need a rehearsal or two, but if you can stop your car just a split second before impact, then Bert can roll off your bonnet and straight under the wheels – great, eh?'

My mind raced quickly over everything that I had been taught on my advanced driving courses. I could now comfortably tail a bandit car at seventy miles an hour through a crowded city centre. I could accelerate around the tightest of corners as if I was running on a rail. I could even negotiate a sideways skid on a wet greasy road. But what the hell do I do when a lunatic kamikaze caretaker takes a header on to my bonnet with the sole and definite intention of disappearing under my wheels? I could just imagine the attitude of Scotland Yard if the thing went wrong! 'You say, constable, that in an effort to improve the standard of road safety you ran down this Bert – a much-loved caretaker – in front of the whole school? Did you consider this was a major contribution to road safety?'

I was wildly unenthusiastic as I sat myself nervously in my little 1000cc motor car. I waited for a suitable lull in the traffic before I drove apprehensively down Cooks Road. I wondered if my current feeling was similar to that felt by a hired assassin. I could hardly see my intended victim. He was waiting with his back against the wall of a block of flats reading a newspaper. On my approach he was to rush forward to the kerbside. This move would place him instantly behind the parked cars and, therefore, out of my vision. Because I had lost sight of him, I was not even aware which two cars he was to appear between in order to kill himself!

I was just about to stop and cancel the whole thing when I saw Ron with his camera rolling. How about that – I'm an actor too! Come on, Bert, we'll make this death scene so real that the kids will cry for weeks! Suddenly there he was, walking briskly out into my path still reading his damned paper. The thud was terrifying. My wheels had barely ceased rolling before Bert had ricocheted from my bonnet and plunged down out of sight somewhere in front of my car. All my previous fears raced back. I need not have worried. Other than a fair-sized hole in the knee of his trousers, Bert was fine. He certainly looked better than I did.

We premiered our film at the school assembly and felt rather pleased with it. I stood up and asked the children for their opinions.

'Don't you think this film is better than all those other road safety films you have seen?' I asked loadedly.

'Y-e-s!' they all chorused.

'Why is that, do you think?' I persisted, confidently expecting the well-it-is-round-here-and-this-is-where-we-live type of rejoinder.

'Because Mr Appleton was killed!' came back the cheering response from every wretched kid in the hall.

I suddenly wondered if we had it quite right.

15. Just a couple of flutters

My personal radio sputtered into life. '604, 604, ring your wife at home. Urgent. Repeat – urgent!' Now there's a message to turn the stomach. All sorts of disasters leap to mind. The fact that Joan was never a person to panic made it worse. If she said it was urgent, urgent it would be. Receiving the message was one thing, finding an unvandalized phone was quite another. I finally settled on walking to the station some fifteen minutes away.

'It's your dad,' she said, in response to my anxious questions. 'Your mother phoned in a dreadful state. He has severe chest pains and although she sent for the doctor over two hours ago, so far no one has called.'

My parents' home was a fifteen-floor council flat in Bermondsey. It was some eight miles from my home but barely five minutes' drive from my police station. A few minutes later I emerged from the lift and let myself into their one-bedroomed flat. My father was ashen and writhing on the bed drenched in sweat. He had aged ten years since I had seen him the previous week. I had never heard him make a complaint but then, between breathless groans, he made his first. 'It's a bit of a sod, Harry,' he panted. 'It really is.' For my dad that was a declaration of monumental agony.

First-aid had never been my forte, but even I knew a heart attack when I saw one. My first task was to hide my shock. My father was a very fit sixty-seven-year-old. Although a heavy smoker, he walked miles every day, carried no surplus weight and had always enjoyed very good health. My mother was beside herself with anxiety.

May Cronin, her good friend of many years, was making brave efforts to comfort her. A few minutes later the arrival of the doctor put the whole emergency system into operation and soon Dad lay in the intensive-care unit at Guy's Hospital.

Mum, May and I sat for hours in that sparse waiting room before the doctor gave us a preliminary report, which, though vague, reassured my mother. Dad, it seemed, was suffering from a fluttering in the chest, caused no doubt by overexcitement. Well, I had to admit he had certainly been very keyed up. Only days earlier he had retired after fifty-five years of work. He and my mother were flying out to visit my brother Stan in Australia just a few days before Christmas, still three weeks away. A twelve-thousand-mile jet trip would unquestionably be the most exciting thing that had happened to the pair of them.

'This condition is not unusual in such cases,' explained the doctor. 'Flutters like this can occur with anyone from time to time. Of course, he won't be able to make the journey to Australia. Well, not at least for a few months anyway. But perhaps around Easter, who knows . . . ?'

Although my mother was reassured, May was most definitely not. I could see by her face that she shared my scepticism. On the first occasion that I found myself alone after this reassurance, I was recalled quickly into the doctor's office. 'I'm sorry,' he said. 'But it's only a question of days, really. A week at the outside. He's had a massive heart attack and there is nothing we can do except make him comfortable.'

Although I had realized the illness was more than a 'flutter' I still felt totally devastated. 'Why?' I heard myself saying. He had worked hard all his life and had been devoted, conscientious and honest. Yet now, two weeks into his retirement, he was going to die. He was going to die and I was going to have to watch him without betraying a word of my knowledge to my mother. I overcame this problem in the only way I knew how. For the fourteen days that my father was to linger, I stopped speaking to her. My entire vocabulary was to consist of little except a few grunts and nods. Meanwhile I declined the offer of compassionate leave from work. The thought of days as well as nights with that self-imposed silence while alone with my mother was unbearable. I needed to work and be alone with my thoughts in those comfortable old Walworth streets.

Because my parents' flat was so close to the hospital, I slept on their living-room floor. This was no easy decision because I was worried about my own house which, due to some rebuilding, consisted at the back entirely of one sheet of plastic. To make things worse, the whole city was experiencing power-cuts because of one strike, and an absence of petrol because of another. Then, just to pile on the agony, the trains in south-east London stopped running. As if in despair, my father gave up and died.

His timing could have been better. It was to be the only night that I had spent away from my mother's flat since the beginning of his illness. It was also 1.30 a.m. on a bitter winter's morning. I was so punch-drunk from lack of sleep that when the hospital rang I unforgivably asked why people only died at inconvenient times. It always seemed to be in the early hours and in the depths of winter. Did no one ever die at midday, I asked, and in the height of summer?

How, I wondered, was I to tell my mother? I had barely spoken to her for a fortnight and now I had to tell her that her husband was dead. In my years on the beat I had broken that news to scores of women, yet why did I have no idea how to approach my own mother? The only tears that I ever shed for my father were on that short lonely drive to break the news of his death. I felt guilty about that. It wasn't much to show for his sixty-seven years.

There can be few more pathetic journeys than to collect the belongings of a dead loved one. It was a little after daybreak as my mother and I walked through the hospital gates. The sleet and rain of the previous weeks had given way to a cold clear winter's morning. The sun had risen over the nearby docks and I suddenly realized this would be the first day in my whole life that my father did not see.

At first it seemed that my father's death was also to deprive my mother of her chance to see her Australian grandchildren. However, Stan agreed to return for the cremation, and we both hoped that we could persuade my mother to accompany him back for a long holiday. My joy at seeing him after so many years was obviously marred by the occasion. He, poor soul, had left the height of a Melbourne summer and travelled half the world to attend a funeral in strike-bound, sleet-covered, trainless London. Having spent just four days with us, half of which was in bed through jet lag, he had then to spend the next two – Christmas Day and Boxing Day – on another jet going home!

It seemed that nothing about my father's death was run to course. Because of the strikes, traffic was horrendous. After a short service at Charterhouse Boys' Club, insufficient time had been allowed to make the eight-mile journey to the crematorium. Unlike the customary snail's pace of a hearse, the one carrying my father's body went away like a rocket. It jumped traffic lights and cut across pavements. The crematorium closed at 4 p.m. and the hearse arrived with just seconds to spare – which is more than can be said for several of the mourners! There were a few indignant complaints from the family – but none from my brother and me. We knew the old man would have loved it!

Stan's few days passed all too quickly and on Christmas Eve I drove both him and my mother to the airport. It was by then early evening with Christmas some six hours away. I had bought neither card nor present. We said our farewells and as the plane lights faded into the distance I experienced an overpowering sense of relief. Had it been only three weeks? It had seemed like ten years. Still, it was finally over and it *was* Christmas. The one present I really wanted was a week's sleep. I was already beginning to miss my father and I idly wondered what next Christmas would be like without him. It was as well I did not know!

Our last football match before Christmas the year after my father died resulted in a particularly fine win. The opponents had been useful but there was no doubt that my team had played really well. It was the sort of game that gave me a glow and set me in good humour for all the following week. The task of running football teams, however, does not end with the final whistle. There are results to phone through, team cards to complete, balls and corner flags to be collected and, with the second XI playing as well, twenty-two sweaty, muddy shirts to be washed. It was rare for both my first and second teams to be playing at the same recreation ground and it had certainly saved a great deal of administration and expense. All in all, I felt, it had been a rather good day.

As I returned home along the A20 I thought back to the same time twelve months before. My mother, now back from Australia, was due to stay with us. Between us all we would each make up for the sadness of the previous year. Some two miles from home I found myself surprised at the sudden change in temperature. That December afternoon had been almost muggy. A soft, steady rain had fallen and the unseasonable 52 degrees Fahrenheit had surprised everyone. Yet there I was, less than an hour after the final whistle, switching the car heater to maximum to keep out the penetrating night chill. Not only was it cold, but it was becoming colder by the minute. By the time I reached home I was positively freezing.

As soon as I entered my front door I laid a searching hand on the passageway radiator. It was cold. 'Why on earth haven't we got the heating on?' I complained irritably.

'Heating on?' echoed Joan. 'But it's so close and humid. It's more like June than December.'

'Talk sense!' I snorted. 'It's bloody perishing out there.'

Within an hour the central heating was rocking full blast. I sat fully dressed in front of the dining-room gas fire, cocooned in two blankets. Still I shivered. My family, of course, wilted. In addition to the cold, there was a constriction around my chest that made me breathless. It was not exactly a pain, more like an extremely tight waistcoat.

'I think it's time to call a doctor,' Joan suggested.

'Why?'

'Oh come on! To be as cold as you are on a day as warm as this can't possibly be right, now can it?'

'Look, I know exactly what this is.' I explained as if to an infant: 'I've had it before. It's just a touch of bronchitis. If you call in a doctor all he will do is to tell me to go to bed and to keep the room warm. I can work that out for myself.'

She sighed in resignation.

Twenty minutes later, following on my own diagnosis and recommended treatment, I retired to my bed in the approved statutory warm room. Well perhaps not 'warm'. Joan claimed it was 'bloody hot'. To me it was an igloo. The constriction around my chest worsened and breathing became even more difficult. Eventually, somewhere around four o'clock I fell asleep. Next morning, however, I felt a little better. This improvement continued throughout the day. By Monday morning I was well enough to attend surgery.

'Yes, Mr Cole, what can I do for you?' asked my GP.

'Touch of bronchitis, Doctor. It's left me a bit breathless with a hell of a chill.'

Three-quarters of an hour later, and bewildered by events, I lay in the casualty cubicle at Lewisham Hospital. Any lingering doubts that remained concerning bronchitis were soon dispelled by the boyish-looking house doctor. While perusing his notes he rubbed his chin thoughtfully.

'I don't *think* we'll put you in the intensive care at *this stage*,' he murmured matter-of-factly.

'Intensive –? But I've only got a touch of bronchitis, surely?'

'No one only has a "touch of bronchitis", Mr Cole. Bronchitis is in fact quite serious. In any case you haven't had bronchitis at all. What you've got, or rather what you seem to have had, is a heart attack.'

'A heart attack! Surely not?'

'It would appear so.'

'A slight one?'

He sighed. 'If one cannot have a "touch" of bronchitis, then one most certainly cannot have a "slight" heart attack.'

'But it's Christmas!'

'Yes, boring, isn't it? Unfortunately these things do tend to happen at the most inopportune time.'

'You don't have to tell *me* that,' I responded ruefully. 'But what does this mean? What's going to happen?'

'Well, we'll fix you up with a saline drip and you'll have total rest. There will be tests and medication and we'll keep you under strict observation for a week or so. I'll send a porter along in a few minutes and he'll trundle you up to the ward.' He closed the curtains with a quick practised flourish and left me alone with my thoughts. I groaned with self-pity. Was this going to be the pattern of all my future yuletides?

As I lay waiting for the porter, the curtains parted and a beautiful Asian nurse glided into my cubicle. She was quite the loveliest nurse I had ever seen. 'Mr Cole?' she murmured sensuously. Speechlessly I nodded. Lifting my hand with the utmost grace she put her delicate fingertips to my pulse and inserted a thermometer into my open mouth. Gazing gently down into my eyes she pushed my parted lips together and whispered deliciously, 'Bowels opened, Mr Cole?' After a fragrant minute she withdrew her fingertips and the thermometer. Peeling back the blankets she presented me with what at first glance appeared to be an off-white, elongated pudding-cloth.

'I'll just slip this nightgown on for you,' she sighed. 'It'll make you feel more comfortable.'

How anyone so beautiful could bring themselves to even handle such a garment amazed me. She draped the thing over my bare shoulders and midriff and tied it loosely around the nape of my neck. Easing me back on to the couch she smoothed my forehead with her cool hand. I remember wondering if they kept her solely for patients who were about to die. 'I won't be long, Mr Cole,' she said musically as she slipped through the curtains.

For the next ten minutes I stared expectantly at those green drapes until footsteps finally approached. Once more they were whisked aside and I lifted my poor frail body towards my angel of mercy. Unfortunately beauty had gone; two beasts stood in her place. The first was a beer-bellied, bewhiskered Scotsman and the second was a greasy-haired, spotty-faced Irishman. 'Dinna worry, auld fella, ye'll be grand in nae time.'

Old fella? I was forty-four! I was more alarmed by the porter's reassuring words than anything that had taken place to date. Five minutes later I was wheeled into B5 ward and placed in the number-one spot by sister's office. That settled it – another Christmas cremation! Well, this time Stan will have to get himself from Melbourne!

Much to everyone's relief – particularly mine and my brother's – I improved greatly. Within a day or so I had already discovered the biggest problem to being in hospital over Christmas – the visitors! There is a never-ending stream of people who feel duty-bound to call. In my case most of them were in police uniform; sympathy, therefore, was at a premium. This was best typified by the forbidding first words of my old friend Danny Cooke.

'Don't you die, you bastard,' he snapped. 'You owe me three quid!'

Perhaps the main advantage of any Christmas incarceration is the goodies that are brought in. Grapes and oranges are out. Booze becomes the order of the day. My locker contained scotch, gin, sherry, port and red wine. There may have been the statutory fruit bowl on top of the locker, but underneath it looked like a brewery. The patients swopped and sampled each other's drinks to such an extent that it was rumoured each saline drip contained vodka.

All good things come to an end and on New Year's day I was finally released. After a short spell as an out-patient I attended for my last appointment.

'I think you're fine now, Mr Cole. If you have any more problems don't hesitate to get straight back in touch with us. Meanwhile, do you have any questions you wish to ask?'

'You bet! How did this happen and where does this leave me?'

'Well, I'm pretty sure you had a slight flutter as a direct result of delayed reaction to the death of your father. There appears to be no other reason. This simply leaves you very much as you were. You can go from here and do just about anything you feel capable of doing. Just don't do anything silly, that's all.'

Bright and early next morning I returned to work. 'The chief superintendent wants to see you in his office,' I was told, almost before I had walked through the station door. 'Oh, and by the way,' added the station officer, 'we've had a new one since you've been away. Cracknell's his name.'

'What's he like, sarge?'

'First impressions – not bad, I'd say.'

Chief Superintendent John Cracknell was just about the most immaculately turned-out copper I ever saw. He offered me a seat and enquired as to my health.

'Fine, sir.'

'You've been on the streets for twenty-two years now?'

I nodded.

'Perhaps it's time you came in out of the rain. How would you like an inside posting?'

'I wouldn't.'

'Why?'

'I don't honestly know why. I just wouldn't, that's all. Why can't I stay where I am?'

'But you can! I don't particularly want to move you but they are the streets and anything can happen out there. I just want to be sure that you feel you could cope.' He rose and walked across the room to the window. His top-floor office commanded a good view across the rooftops of south-east London. 'Come here a moment.' As I joined him at the window he pointed generally through the glass. 'What do you see out there?'

I was not yet sure of the point he was making and was distrustingly vague in my reply. 'Streets?'

'Precisely! Streets! And how long have they been there?'

I shrugged. 'One – two hundred years maybe?'

'That's quite correct. They were here yesterday and they'll be here tomorrow and doubtless they will remain here for another one to two hundred years. They will be here whether you walk them or not. Never forget that. If you feel even remotely bad –' he turned from the view and looked me directly in the eyes – 'go home. If anyone asks you why you are going, then refer them to me – understand?'

I could not believe I was hearing correctly. A new chief superintendent laying his head on the line for a PC he had never even met before! I was so grateful I had to struggle for words, yet it was important to me that I found them. Finally I composed myself. 'Yes I understand, I understand very well. I appreciate what you have just said more than anything else that has been said to me since I joined this force. Thank you.' I deliberately avoided the word 'sir'. Its inclusion would have smacked of obligation. Its exclusion was the highest compliment I could pay him. Within a week I was to doubt the wisdom of refusing his offer.

'Harry,' the station officer said, 'go and have a look at that number 12 bus outside. The conductor reckons there's a stroppy drunk on the top deck who's frightening all the passengers. Give a shout if you need any help – all right?'

'All right, sarge.'

The request was an absolute stone-bonker run-of-the-mill disturbance call. It was food and drink to a street copper. I was so used to it I could have dealt with it in my sleep. Unfortunately I was very much awake. I was not only awake but I was nervous and apprehensive. Very slowly I climbed those thirteen stairs to the top of the bus. He was on the third seat along and his legs sprawled across the gangway. In spite of the chill day he was stripped to the waist. A variety of bizarre tattoos covered most of his torso. He was not particularly big but big enough to be a handful. He was not particularly drunk but drunk enough to be dangerous. He was not particularly aggressive, but aggressive enough to need watching.

'Whadder you fuckin' want?' he asked.

I could feel myself shaking. I tried my standby line for such situations. It had worked numerous times before. 'Right, c'mon, mate, last one off the bus is a cissy. Ready, steady –' I made no attempt to finish, I could see it was futile. I realized that in order to carry off that particular approach one needed to be totally relaxed and confident. I was neither. Even a drunk would see through it. 'If you need any help,' the station officer had said – I reached for my radio.

The young PC who hurried to assist me looked about twelve years old. He dragged the man downstairs and off the bus with little or no effort.

'Are you going to charge him or shall I?' he asked.

I breathlessly raised both my hands and shook my head: 'You . . . please,' I panted.

Stumbling to the canteen, I fell into the first chair I saw. I could not believe it, my nerve had gone. A tuppenny-ha'penny drunk had put the fear of Christ up me and I was scared witless. I had eight years to go in the job; was this, then, what it was always going to be like? I had never felt so low. I honestly believed my problem was in the mind but

I had no idea how to cope. Consulting the police medical officer at twenty-two years' service struck me as too great a risk. The very least he would do would be to farm me away to some office. The more likely result would be to discharge me on medical grounds. I wanted neither.

This indecision, to say nothing of the fear, was to continue for two months before it was resolved by pure chance. Since my illness, although I had continued to run my Saturday football club, I had lost interest in my station team. It was by then the last week in April and they were due to play their final match of a very indifferent season. 'Why don't you come along?' said the secretary. 'We'll adjourn for a few jars afterwards and kid ourselves we'll do better next year.'

Plumstead Common on a cold wet April afternoon is *not* Wembley Stadium. The wind cuts up from the Thames marshes and whistles through the slits and cracks of the shedlike changing rooms. The cold showers seek out every bruised and aching muscle. Players do not fall over themselves to play here even at the height of the season. A late April fixture with nothing at stake requires more motivation than the average club secretary is capable of. My team had nine players, the opponents' had ten. I was faced with a decision. Stand and watch and be bored or frozen to death – or play and listen anxiously to each heartbeat. There was no decision to make really. I had changed within minutes.

In the pub afterwards most players agreed that the nil-nil draw had been the worst game of the season. I was the lone dissenter. I thought it had been a marvellous match and I could not wait for next September.

16. The seventh ball

'I suppose now you're a proper FA coach, you consider yourself too good for the poor old station team, is that it?' Inspector Andrew Goodyear had been 'persuaded' by the superintendent to manage the station football team and he was not overhappy about the prospect. I had run the side for some years but there was no doubt that an inspector could 'arrange' duties for key players in a way that was completely beyond the powers of a mere constable. In fact I had not refused to *play* for the side at all, I had simply refused to *coach* it. With Charterhouse Boys' Club taking two of my evenings and a half of my Saturday I simply could not spare the time.

'It's not what you think, guv',' I explained. 'My coaching is aimed at teenagers who can improve, not thirty-two-year-old ball-belting wrestlers who are beyond redemption. I'll tell you what I will do, though,' I offered, desperately seeking a compromise. 'I'll write a little constructive account of each game and pin it up on the canteen noticeboard, how about that?'

'It's better than nothing, I suppose,' muttered Andrew grudgingly, 'although I don't see how that is going to affect the half of the team that can't read.'

In all honesty I thought I had got out rather well. I had no conception of the monster I had created. The average police-station football team consists of two – maybe three – very useful players, three – even four – keen, chase-the-ball-everywhere-but-never-quite-get-it players, and then there is the rest. The last group will certainly be clad in football gear, and will be taking part in a football match.

On occasions they may even come into contact with the ball, but footballers they are not and never will be as long as they have holes in their ears. If they were coached twelve hours a day, seven days a week, they would still not improve. They will continue to play what is referred to in coaching circles as a 'hard useless game'.

The first thing I discovered from writing these weekly bulletins was that people in the last group were the keenest to read about themselves. Each week, therefore, in addition to the match account and a résumé of the more technical side of the game, I found I was required to write another eleven paragraphs concerning the individual players. This is fine if there is something to say, but there were always at least two players whom I never realized were even *with* us until I met them in the bar afterwards.

By coincidence, it was around this time that Sergeant Peter Simmons took over the editorship of the *Warren* magazine. The *Warren* was a house magazine for the whole of south-east London police force. The publication had been good even before Peter's arrival, but under his guidance it blossomed into a very good journal indeed. Purely on the basis of my fictional football accounts, I was given a regular column in the *Warren* where I was allowed to write about the more idiotic or even bizarre side of the force. (This at times even included my family!)

I had been writing the column for some years when in July 1978 I received a letter from a Superintendent Summerville from Rochester Row Police Station.

'I read the enclosed story in the Russell Harty column in the *Observer*,' wrote the superintendent, 'and I thought it sounded rather familiar. I therefore looked up an old copy of the *Warren* magazine. Perhaps you should do the same. I'm sure you'll find it of interest,' he concluded.

I read the story. It was familiar all right. I had written the same story – almost word for word – in the magazine some time earlier. Fame indeed! My first words in a national newspaper! Well, not under my name, of course, but nevertheless, *my* story. I was so pleased that I wrote to the *Observer* immediately and congratulated them on their good taste. I also suggested that if they needed any more of the same I would certainly come cheaper than Russell. They refused this rather generous gesture and killed the whole business stone-dead by promising that they would 'look into the matter'. In newspaper parlance this meant that I would never hear another word about it.

This incident certainly bolstered my confidence and my contributions to the *Warren* took on a new impetus. Sadly, no matter how thoroughly I studied the *Observer* after that date, no one else showed the same good sense that Russell Harty had.

Just as my enthusiasm was waning, a second coincidence took place. Tony Parker, the professional writer of books, radio and television plays, came to research material on my home beat. Tony asked me for a prolonged interview on my view of the area as seen through the eyes of a policeman. After two one-hour interviews, with Tony asking all the questions, I slipped in one of my own. I dumped a great pile of *Warren* magazines in front of him and watched his face fall.

'D'you reckon I could do a book? If you tell me "No", I won't mind,' I lied.

'I'll give you my opinion – nothing else,' he offered.

It sounded fair to me, and off he went staggering under the weight of his Japanese tape recorder and eight years' supply of my magazines.

A week later I saw him again.

'Write me two chapters, will you? But they must be honest,' he insisted.

'Honest?'

'Yes, you know, what *you* feel, how *you* actually see the police force. After twenty-six years you must have an opinion. Okay, then let's hear it.'

At first this idea totally threw me. I had certainly written my column that way but that was for a more or less captive audience. It seemed that every police book, film or play that I had ever seen was pure cops-and-robbers. It was straight up he-did-it-and-I-caught-him stuff. How, then, was I to begin to write a police book if (a) I did not know who 'he' was in the first place, and (b) I never looked like catching him in the second? More than somewhat perplexed, I went away and began work on the two requested chapters.

'Can you finish a book by the end of the year?' subsequently asked agent Abner Stein.

'Of course I can,' I assured him, not letting on that it took me three months to write an answering letter to my brother in Australia.

'Then we are in business,' he replied.

This urgency was all very well but there was one great fat fly in the ointment – Scotland Yard. No constable since 1829 had written a commercial book about the force while still a serving member. Policemen and writers were an antithesis as far as the Yard was concerned. I could of course resign before publication but this would mean leaving the force after twenty-seven years' service with an appreciable loss of pension rights. I decided to take a chance. I submitted a copy of the manuscript to Scotland Yard at the same time as I submitted one to the publishers.

The result amazed me. Not only did the force raise no objections (except for two slight administrative corrections) but they were so much in favour of it that they requested permission to use extracts for recruiting purposes! I had barely recovered from that when I was invited to the police Senior Staff College at Bramshill to give a talk to their literary society! This is the equivalent of a cookhouse private lecturing at Sandhurst.

Like all new writers, I looked forward eagerly to my first publication date. A few months before this actual day, the proofs were sent to me for correction. They arrived on Friday and were due back the following Wednesday. In the meantime my May Day Monday leave was cancelled.

'Sorry, Harry,' said the duty sergeant, 'but I've got to provide twenty blokes for reserve-duty at the Iranian Embassy siege.'

'What do we do there, sarge?'

'Not a lot, just sit on the coach all day and get bored to death, usually.'

'Are you really sure we do nothing else?'

'We haven't done so far.'

'Great! It's just what I need! Can I sit on the coach and correct my proofs and get Bank Holiday rates of pay for it?'

'You can stand naked on your head and whistle "God Save the Queen" as long as you're on that coach,' he answered with an indifferent shrug.

Monday, 5 May was a very sunny day in Knightsbridge but it was also very cold. I was quite happy when in the early afternoon our coach pulled into Albert Court, a quiet little sidestreet at the rear of the Albert Hall where we were scheduled to remain until relieved at 7 p.m.

'Right! Make yourselves comfortable, lads,' ordered the inspector in charge. 'You're here for the next few hours. If you really *must* go to the toilet then creep into the stage-door of the Albert Hall opposite.'

Our coach was only half full so I spread myself and my papers across a double seat.

Before I began to read the manuscript, I and several of my colleagues decided that we would use the facilities of the stage-door lavatory across the road. It was while I stood facing that chipped glazed wall that I became aware of some familiar notes of music. Quickly zipping up, I went in search of it. Along a short corridor, up two flights of stairs and behind a drawn curtain, there it was. I softly pulled back the curtain and found myself practically on stage. Helen Reddy and a small musical group were rehearsing for that very evening's concert. I could not believe my luck! First I was checking my proofs and receiving double-time, and now a free concert at the same rate! Fortunately our inspector was also a fan and he showed great tolerance for those of us who were to remain transfixed with Miss Reddy for so long on that vast empty stage.

A little after six o'clock, with rehearsals now finished, I made my way once more to the coach and began to reassemble my papers. I had just begun to make myself comfortable when a series of shots were heard. At first there was confusion but the inspector's radio soon spluttered into life.

'Everyone out! They're going to storm the embassy!'

'But –' I began. I was about to say, 'They can't – I have some proofs to correct,' when I thought better of it.

'You were going to say something?' asked the inspector, with one ear tilted into his personal radio.

'Not really, guv',' I replied. 'Except that I'm wondering whether coppering and writing are going to mix.' As it transpired, I later came to think I was not the only one who believed this. I am sure that most of the media people sent to interview me *firmly* believed it.

The fact that they had stumbled across a street copper who could string three words together seemed to throw them into utter confusion. They had firmly believed that a constable's main tasks were to open doors for detective inspectors and make the tea in television plays. During these interviews I realized that in spite of the thousands of words and miles of film about the police churned out by these people, they never really knew us at all.

There was, however, one stage in these interviews when my nerve really failed me. I had been invited to appear on the Russell Harty book programme that was to be recorded on a Sunday afternoon at the Television Centre at White City. Russell Harty! I could not believe my luck. I could not wait to present him with 'our' original story.

'How will you travel?' the programme secretary asked. 'Will you come in your own car or would you like us to send you a taxi?'

'Who pays for it?'

'We do, of course.'

'I'll come by taxi!' A taxi! I would only travel by taxi if I had an hour to live; even then my demise would have been hastened by the shock of watching the meter. Yet there I was being offered the chance to ride across London and back at someone else's expense! To me life had no greater luxury, I gloried in it.

As I crossed central London that wet July day, I remembered all the times when I had been on a traffic point with the rain flooding out of my socks. It was on those occasions that I had really envied people who were so blasé about riding in cabs that they actually sat and read – some even dozed – in them. It was now my turn and I searched each junction for the sight of some bedraggled, harassed copper sorting out a tangled traffic jam. Sadly it wasn't to be. It really is true, you *never* can find a policeman when you want one!

With my customary unpunctuality, I arrived late and missed the rehearsal. This obviously worried the producer but with time so short there was little that could be done about it. I joined the rest of the guests for a rather lavish buffet and sat myself down with a generous salad opposite a distinguished elderly gentleman. I use the word 'distinguished' because everyone seemed to fawn upon him. He was obviously a man of some consequence.

'Who are you and what are you doing here today?' he suddenly asked.

I told him my name and my purpose and he introduced himself. It was then I discovered that the world is divided into two camps, those that know Dr A. L. Rowse and those that have never heard of him. I was amongst the latter. I had nodded politely when he had introduced himself, but when he added, 'You must forgive me but I've never heard of you,' it seemed only courteous to reply, 'Don't worry, I've never heard of you either.' I certainly had no idea of the effect this response would produce. 'Never heard of me! Never heard of me!' he echoed. 'I just happen to be the greatest living authority on Shakespeare and Elizabethan England. Even in America I am known from coast to coast!'

'Well, I'm truly sorry, but I originate from Bermondsey and I've never heard of you.'

For some reason he seemed to regard this admission as a challenge and for the next fifteen minutes he proceeded to give me the benefit of his views on most subjects. There was certainly no shortage of them – either views or subjects – and I found myself in friendly disagreement with most of them.

'Dr Rowse!' interrupted one of the assistants. 'Time for make-up, Doctor.'

'I'll not go unless this young man accompanies me,' he insisted.

I began to warm to him. Young man, eh? He was obviously far more astute than I had first credited.

It was while we were at make-up that my day's highlight was reached. The door of the room was thrown open and the writer Leslie Thomas entered, glass in hand. 'Dr Rowse!' he exclaimed. 'May I compliment you on your excellent biography of Brunel?'

Now I am badly enough read to be classified as illiterate, but even I knew Rowse had not written on Brunel.

'Thank you for your kind words,' said the Doctor huffily, 'but I am afraid I did not have the privilege of writing that book. It was written in fact by my good friend L. T. C. Rolt.'

'I'm sorry,' apologized the intruder, pivoting on his heels. 'I'll go out and come in again.'

I glanced across at the Doctor. His face was plastered with a sand-like substance.

'You know you haven't had a very good day, have you?' I asked. 'First I didn't know you from Adam, and now you've just been complimented on a book you didn't write.'

He responded with a smile that seemed to indicate that

he had actually enjoyed this affront to his regality.

'Come along, gentlemen,' announced the floor assistant. 'Mr Harty is waiting to introduce you to the audience.'

We passed along a short, carpeted corridor into the side of a hangar-like studio. We paused for a moment in the wings while Russell Harty, in a beautiful suit, finished a very smooth patter to the audience.

'You know what I most admire about Russell?' the Doctor asked suddenly. I was surprised at his tone. I had a feeling that he was about to deliver a compliment and I would think that was a very rare phenomenon.

'What?' I asked, genuinely curious.

'His ability to keep six balls in the air at the same time.'

I knew exactly what he meant. The man was a sheer professional. I fingered the article in my pocket. Okay, it appeared under his name. So what? The story could have been picked up from anywhere. He may not even have seen it until after he had signed it. After all, this *was* my first book and I was actually appearing on *his* programme. That made us level, surely? As if to bear out my decision, Harty made the filming particularly easy for me. Two hours later I climbed into my taxi for the journey home. The return trip was a pleasing yet unrewarding one. Again, I never clapped eyes on a policeman.

17. Some senior officers

A widespread misapprehension about the police force –
most commonly held by those who have just been arrested
– is that a police officer's promotion is governed by the
number of arrests he or she makes. If this were taken to its
logical conclusion, then Commissioners would be the
world's unparalleled thief-takers. In reality, it is doubtful
whether any Commissioner arrested more than a handful
of people throughout his whole career.

Promotion within the Metropolitan Police – certainly up
to the rank of inspector – is governed solely by the results
of a competitive exam. If you are good enough you will
pass, if you are not you won't. This system means that
going around arresting people can be quite detrimental to
promotion prospects: an ambitious young constable who
spends half of his week in court instead of studying is
unlikely to make sergeant without several attempts at the
exam.

The first step to sergeant can be taken after three years.
Beginning each spring, weekly promotion classes are held.
The applicant will then need to give every minute of his
spare time to studying for the exam the following year.
Pretty much the same system applies at the next stage, from
sergeant to inspector. Advancement beyond that rank,
however, is by selection. (It was at this stage that it was
once considered an advantage to be a freemason.)

This system has worked fairly well over the decades but
it does have flaws. A police officer who is good at exams
does not necessarily make a good senior copper.
Frequently the reverse is the case. The most noticeable

flaw is in the question of decisions. 'Don't make decisions and you won't make a wrong one' is a well-tried philosophy. An excellent illustration of this was given by an inspector friend of mine a few weeks before I retired from the force.

Inspector George Mitchell had been on a refresher 'shield training' course for a couple of days. This course sets up extremely real-life situations in which a copper finds himself being bombarded with bricks, concrete and other missiles. The idea is that the victims will then be compelled to work as a unit, their combined shields taking the brunt of the attack. Having spent a very hairy period as the target, George quite relished the idea of his turn as the freedom-fighter hurling the bricks.

After gleefully letting rip with two or three small chunks of concrete, George realized that he had torn his duty gloves. (This apparel was a pure status symbol: inspectors wore gloves, PCs used bare hands.) On returning to the station he submitted a report for a new pair. He made the sensible request that he be allowed to keep the old pair to prevent a recurrence at any future freedom-fighting. This simple request was made on a single form. Three months later a whole fat file thudded into his tray. In twelve weeks George's request had made the rounds of fourteen different administrators. Each one gave careful consideration to it, added his own recommendations, then passed it on to someone else for a decision! The fourteenth person had actually *made* a decision. 'No,' he stated, George could *not* keep his old gloves!

'You'll never make superintendent,' the old PCs had prophetically said in my youth, 'if you go around making decisions.'

These promotion exams, being so closely based on text-book theory, can ignore the one requirement which a police officer needs more than any other – that of common sense. Ninety-five per cent of all street-duty *is* common sense. Knowing when to shout and when to whisper, what to see and what to miss, what to hear and what to not quite catch, that is a street-skill that comes with experience. If this ability could be allied to the promotion theory then one would truly have a remarkable senior officer.

A superintendent who was particularly short on this requirement was on duty outside Westminster Abbey at the funeral of Lord Mountbatten. He caused me great apprehension. We had paraded for duty at five o'clock that morning. Having been to a party the night before, I was not too distressed to discover we were on reserve in a coach just around the corner from the Abbey. I sprawled across two seats, put my brain into neutral and went out like a light.

'All outside! All outside! C'mon, wake up there. Just because you are on reserve does not mean you can slump all over the coach. I have an urgent job for you men.'

I awoke through bleary eyes to see a bumptious, panic-stricken superintendent shouting at everyone in general and me in particular. Playing-cards were stashed away, helmets sought and yawns stifled.

'Quickly, now, we have a security task,' he persisted.

Still adjusting our buttons, we were led around the corner towards a large group of quiet, well-dressed, middle-aged and elderly people who were covering most of the pavement near the entrance to the Abbey.

'These people are not allowed there and they will have to be moved. This section of footway must be kept clear throughout the entire ceremony for security reasons.'

'You can't move these, guv'!' I exclaimed. 'In the first place they won't move and in the second place, they will be so insulted they will probably lynch you – or even worse – us!'

'My orders are that this pavement must be kept clear for security reasons and *kept* clear it will be. Now move them off!'

I was not sure what my position would be for 'refusing

to obey a lawful order'. I was just weighing up all the possibilities when we were dealt a sudden reprieve. Like a God-sent branch of the 7th Cavalry, Commander John Cracknell (formerly a chief superintendent at my own station) appeared on a horse. I almost ran to meet him.

'Guv'nor,' I blurted, 'there are about sixty former members of Mountbatten's Chindit army over there, some with their wives, and we've been told to remove them on grounds of *security*! They'll go mad!'

The Commander nodded. 'They probably will,' he agreed.

He turned his mount towards them and bade them all a general 'Good morning, ladies and gentlemen'. Addressing himself to the apparent leader he continued, 'You can all stay. All I ask is that you remain in position until the ceremony is over.'

The situation was instantly defused but the possibilities had been frightening. Half the world's television cameras were trained on that location. If we had attempted to move the group there would have been hell to pay. Each of those Chindits understandably assumed they had as much right to be there – outside on the pavement – as many members of the congregation who were inside the Abbey. I knew this, the youngest PC in our group knew this. The only person who seemed unaware of it was the superintendent who had called us from the coach in the first place.

Perhaps the problem of indecision in the intermediate ranks has not been assisted by successive Commissioners. I served under six and with just one exception I felt as removed from each of them as I am from the Pope. I spent thirty years within a mile and a half of Scotland Yard and apart for the odd ceremonial occasion, I never saw one of them! Commissioners to me were nothing but figureheads. They played no real part in my life. The exception to this rule was Robert Mark. Mark actually stood up and said things. I always had the feeling that his appointment had been a fortunate mistake. I am sure if it had been known how strong-willed he was he would never have been offered the position. This theory was borne out after his departure when there was an immediate return to the anonymity of previous Commissioners.

Perhaps because I rarely saw a Commissioner I am not a suitable person to judge one. The same could not be said for the intermediate ranks. Up until the seventies, most police stations were the responsibility of a superintendent. An extra rank was then introduced and many of these men were promoted to chief superintendent on the spot. In addition, they were given a deputy, a superintendent who had been newly promoted from chief inspector. These two men, plus the occasional glimpse of the District Commander, are the only senior officers that the average copper ever sees, so it is on them that he will, rightly or wrongly, form an opinion of all senior ranks. These two senior men owe their positions not to any great policing ability, but because they are supposedly good administrators. This system means that, with a few notable exceptions, the higher a person goes in the rank structure, the more removed they become from the street realities of present-day policing.

We actually had one superintendent at Carter Street who, having managed to persuade the Surveyor's Department to carpet the front office, decided that it looked so nice that PCs and sergeants should be prohibited from walking upon it. He therefore banned everyone who was not actually posted to the front office from entering the place! The fact that every PC and sergeant on duty *needed* to enter two or three times a day was a mere bagatelle. No pudden-footed copper was going to scuff up the pile on his brand-new carpet and he flooded the station with memos to that effect.

It may have been twenty years since some of these superintendents pounded a beat and a street copper's life would have changed out of all recognition within that time. To be fair, most have adapted extremely well, and the old-style crime-busting, lead-from-the-front guv'nors hardly exist. At one time, when an area had a particularly high street-crime rate, the superintendent would send out half a dozen of his best thief-takers with the brief instruction, 'Fetch a few in.' That attitude began to change in the seventies, as I discovered for myself in 1972, when I was on duty in Whitehall during a protest march about the 1972 Immigration Bill.

'Right, listen!' the stern-faced chief superintendent commanded. 'There are about 3000 protesters and they will march down Whitehall and hand a petition in at the Home Office. During this march they will abuse you, spit at you and may even assault you, *BUT* on no account is anyone to be arrested. Understand? No one!'

I never heard it put quite so forthrightly as that again, nevertheless the attitude gathered momentum – albeit more discreetly – throughout the next decade under the guise of 'low-profile'. The peak of this constabulary inactivity is reached of course with the Notting Hill Carnival. This street-crime bonanza must cause old-time coppers to turn in their graves!

Sadly there are some senior officers who can be described by the policeman's poignant moan, 'He might be good on paperwork but he's a windy git and he'll never make a copper as long as he has a hole in his arse.' At my own station we were unfortunate enough to have two of these types in one dual posting. Their effect on morale was devastating. Nothing seemed to matter to them as long as the paperwork was right. They had only been there for a few days before I first ran foul of them.

'Ah-ha! 604!' exclaimed Sergeant Peter Cage as he discovered me in the canteen instead of half a mile away on my beat. 'I have just the undertaking for you.'

I was bang-to-rights and I knew it. I decided to cut the chat and find out what he wanted as soon as possible. This would not be easy, he would deliberately prolong every moment if he thought it would bring me either disadvantage or discomfort.

'What is it, what d'you want done? And why "undertaking"?' I asked, foolishly rising to the bait. 'You're not usually so eloquent. What's the matter with the word "job"?'

'It's "undertaking", Constable Cole, because it is a task from on high. Via the Commissioner no less. There now, you're impressed, I can see.'

'I doubt if this Commissioner could ever impress me,' I replied discourteously. 'Are you going to tell me what this is or not?'

'Well, you have been selected for a special public-relations exercise. It is a problem which has obviously given the Commissioner some worry. Because the Commissioner was worried, the superintendent and the chief superintendent were worried. Now, because I'm a caring young sergeant, I'm worried. Of course you're neither young nor caring but when you read this letter you'll worry too.'

'What about?'

He glanced quickly around the deserted canteen and put a finger to his lips. 'Shssss,' he whispered. 'Graffiti.'

'Graffiti! Where? What about it?'

'The subway at the Elephant and Castle.'

'But it's only the graffiti that keeps the bloody walls up! In any case, what's it to do with me?'

'It's on your beat.'

'It's not.'

'Well, it's close – and it's yours,' he said, as he thrust a file of papers towards me.

I glanced quickly through the file and at first I believed it was a rather weak wind-up. Then I saw a note from the superintendent and I knew that whatever it was it would not be a wind-up. Superintendent Heath did not go in for wind-ups. I read on. There was a copy of an anonymous letter from a gentleman in east Dulwich and it was addressed to Sir David McNee, New Scotland Yard. 'Dear

Sir David, I hope you are well,' it began. Having sought thus to ingratiate himself, the writer then moved on to his main purpose. 'While walking through the Elephant and Castle subway I noticed the graffiti.' How observant, I thought. 'Amongst this graffiti, I spotted the emblem of a swastika. I thought I would report it to you, sir.'

'Is that it?' I asked incredulously.

'Well, that plus the covering memo from Scotland Yard, to say nothing of a similar one from the superintendent. Yes, it is.'

'What am I supposed to do about it?'

'Go and have a look at it.'

'Okay – so I go to the Elephant and Castle subway and amongst all the graffiti I discover this swastika – what then?'

'Mr Heath doesn't say anything about "what then", he just says go and have a look at it. So go and have a look at it.'

I cursed my way to the location and began to read the walls of the subway. I discovered all sorts of astonishing anatomical revelations about many of my young female parishioners and an unbelievable claim by a chap named Big Dick but never a trace of a swastika.

I returned to the station and, having sought out Sergeant Cage, I made my brief verbal report: 'No swastikas.'

'Okay, put it on paper.'

'Don't be silly, sergeant! What's the point of putting it on paper? It's a big nothing, even you must admit that.'

'It may be a big nothing to you and me, Constable Cole, but to Mr Heath it is an assignment of monumental magnitude and he will want a report on everything you found and your actions.'

'I'm not doing it, it's trivia!'

'Of course it's trivia! He loves trivia, it's trivia what keeps him going. Give him a report about trivia and he'll be happy for a week.'

'Right! You're on! I'll give you a report all right! There's just one thing I want to check first, though. Will he require all the details of my search and exactly what I found?'

'Of course, that's what it's all about.'

'Sergeant, if there is one thing you can be really sure of now, it is that you will most definitely get a report.'

'Oh good, I am pleased! I do hope you are not going to become facetious though, constable. Mr Heath would not like that. On the other hand,' he winked, 'I suppose you can only put in the report what your actions were, can't you? I can't see how anyone could possibly criticize you for that.'

An hour later I placed my report in the superintendent's 'in' tray. It read:

Re Attached Complaint from Anonymous Member of the Public Concerning Swastikas at the Elephant and Castle Subway.

Superintendent,

I have searched these subways diligently for two hours and I discovered the following graffiti. Twenty-eight nude women, twenty-five of whom have astonishing physical characteristics. Nine naked men with seventeen erections between them(!). Fifteen copulations. Four slogans stating 'Kill the pigs' and three stating 'All coppers are bastards'.

There were also numerous mentions of Millwall Football Club, The Who and Big Rita from Waterloo who apparently does a turn. (As regards the latter, there was also a bitter complaint from a fellow named Alan who said she gave him the pox.) In spite of this thorough and time-consuming search, I did not discover a swastika. However, should one appear, I will of course give it my undivided attention while keeping an open mind on Big Rita.

It was two days before I had a response. Then, to my

surprise, I was summoned to appear, not before Superintendent Heath, but Chief Superintendent Walters. During these two days, my frustration at the stupidity of the whole situation had subsided. I realized that my report had gone way over the top and I was prepared for an angry reception. To my surprise Walters showed not anger but genuine perplexity.

'I don't think this is the proper way for such reports to be made out, do you?' He shook his head sadly. 'I would have expected a man of your service to have known that.'

'I was sent up to the Elephant and Castle, sir, to perform about the most futile task I have come across since I have been in this job. There is no other police force in the world that would have given that letter, anonymous as it is, more than ten seconds. Yet it has travelled through a dozen hands before it came down to me. The amount of police hours spent on it must be colossal – and for what? We had ten thousand reported crimes at this station last year and I'm sodding about with swastikas!'

'There is a system for dealing with correspondence to the Commissioner, you were simply carrying it out.'

'But it's absolute trivia, sir!'

'I'm a great believer in trivia. You know what they say – "Look after the pennies and the pounds will look after themselves."'

I was left speechless by the comparison but I did manage to leave the office without rewriting the report and soon the whole incident began to slip from my mind. Within a month it was to come crashing back.

The Brixton street riots put an enormous strain on the Metropolitan Police. We were ill-prepared and because of insufficient protection, our casualties were enormous. Stations like my own that bordered on Brixton were stripped bare of policemen, and most of the day-to-day running was left to just a few WPCs who worked anything from twelve to sixteen hours a day.

It was at four in the morning during one of the few quiet

208

spells that Superintendent Heath decided to make a surprise visit to the station. For the first time in twenty-four hours all of the outstanding emergency calls had been cleared and the shift of three officers (instead of fifteen) were at last up to date. To celebrate, the station officer had ordered a brew-up and they were all enjoying a cup of tea. Suddenly the door was thrown open and the superintendent, in full regalia, strode into the front office. He went straight on the attack.

'When you came on duty last night, sergeant, did you sign to say everything was in order?'

'Well – er, yes, yes, I did,' answered the puzzled sergeant.

'And did you inspect everything and make sure it was in order before signing?' (*All* station officers are required to sign on taking over the front office. *None* ever checks, otherwise each changeover would take at least two hours!)

Once more the bewildered station officer bleated out an admission.

'Ah-ha!' exclaimed Heath dramatically. 'Then come with me.'

Leaving the front office, the pair descended the rear steps into the station yard. 'This way,' directed the superintendent. They zig-zagged between the parked police cars before arriving at a ground-floor windowsill. 'There!' boomed Heath, pointing at the sill.

'What about it, sir?' asked the now totally confused sergeant.

'Can't you see it, man? It's a teacup! Yet you claim you checked everything before you signed. You know what this means don't you?'

'Er – no, I'm afraid I don't.'

'It means, sergeant, that that cup was left there by one of your men during the night. This is in direct contravention of my directive concerning station teacups.'

'But I don't have any men on duty, sir. They are all girls.'

'Their sex doesn't matter, man!' Heath exploded. 'The point is they have left the teacup on the windowsill. What other cups have they left around the building – eh? Tell me that. Come on, we'll search and find out.'

The fires in Brixton had barely been quenched. Nearby King's College Hospital was still full of injured police officers, and two slumbering coppers, too tired to go home, lay motionless in the station's darkened snooker room. Nevertheless, showing superb devotion to duty, the superintendent determinedly led his reluctant sergeant to every corner of the building in an all-out quest for teacups.

Eventually this superintendent received his promotion board. He's taking a chance, I thought. There is always the possibility they will certify him. I should have known better – they promoted him.

It was some months before I thought seriously about him again. I was on duty on the terraces at Stamford Bridge for a Chelsea home match. My colleague for the day was a sergeant from another district.

'Here!' he snapped suddenly, having glanced at the divisional number on my shoulder. 'You're not from Carter Street by any chance, are you?'

I admitted that I was.

'You're the lot who sent us that prat Heath!'

'That's right,' I smiled.

'He's unbelievable, isn't he?'

'Unbelievable is one of his many characteristics – yes.'

'Tell me,' he asked seriously, 'is he barmy?'

'Well, I've got definite views on it, but why do you ask?'

'Well, we were run ragged one day last week. We had a couple of demonstrations that went wrong, bomb threats, a kidnapping and a 'flu epidemic at the nick. It was absolute pandemonium and do you know what he was most worried about?'

'Teacups?'

His mouth and eyes all opened wide. 'How on earth did you know that?'

I winked confidentially. 'That was why I had him moved,' I whispered.

18. The party's over

During my first decade in the force, the anniversary of my entry came around annually. Once past the twenty-year mark it slipped by every four weeks. The years passed at a frightening pace. As I approached the completion of my full service (thirty years), my choice was either to leave, or stay for another two years before a compulsory retirement on the age limit of fifty-five. Although I was tempted to stay, this somehow seemed undignified. It would be like clinging on by my fingertips while waiting for some eagle-eyed administrator to announce I was too old. At the back of my mind was a recollection of the time I had spent looking at a 1912 retirement list. Under the column headed 'Reason for Leaving' the most common cause given was 'Worn Out'! I wanted no teenaged clerical assistant at Scotland Yard sending me such a note. Yet how and when to retire was certainly a problem. Never having been very good with forms, I was suddenly expected to spend hours filling in reams of them in order to resign from a job that I did not want to leave in the first place.

My thirty years was finally reached in December 1982, but I decided I could not possibly leave the job before Christmas. After all, Christmas in the force is such a sociable time. I decided to stay for at least the New Year.

The New Year came and went and so did January and February.

'Hullo, Harry, still here?' friends would say. 'I thought you were going before Christmas.'

'Yes, I – er – was, but I'm – er – going at Easter now.'

I had no idea if I was going at Easter or not. It was simply the next milestone on the calendar.

For three months I woke each morning wondering whether this would be *the* day – the actual day when I would walk into the administration unit and say, 'Give me the forms – I'm going.'

Finally, on Tuesday, 8 March – thirteen weeks later – I just did it. It was as simple as that. However I cannot say I was overhappy with the haste with which the forms were presented to me!

Within minutes the words of a long-retired colleague came flooding back. 'You'll never get out of the force,' he once said. 'You'll never be able to fill in the bloody forms!'

I had assumed he was joking. That was before I had seen them. They were unbelievable! One question asked the current shape of my nose! I can only assume that thirty years in the force changes people's noses. I studied mine intently in the shaving-mirror but it seemed just the same nose I had had when I joined.

The first thing to organize was a party. The problem with any party that involves coppers is finding a civilized time for it. The night-duty has to leave for work around nine-thirty and the late-turn cannot arrive before eleven o'clock. It was therefore no use expecting an orthodox party to be successful. I was saved in this dilemma by a friend who was a groundsman at a south London sports club. 'Why don't you hold it here?' he offered. 'There are no neighbours to worry about and you can go on all night if you like.'

The party was thus taken care of. My next task was to say farewell to all the local people I had known for so long, and to make final visits to the schools.

'You must come in for a farewell school dinner,' announced one headmaster with sadistic glee. 'Of course it won't be your actual lunch at the Ritz – the week before Easter is not the best time to come in – but I'm sure we can rustle you up something.'

'Er – what's the matter with Easter week, then?' I asked apprehensively.

'Well, cook does tend to use up all of those little mysteries that she has accumulated throughout term.' He nodded his head thoughtfully. 'Still, I must say she manages to disguise them pretty well. You can sit in the hall and have lunch with the children. I'm sure they will all enter into the spirit of the thing.'

Entering into the spirit of the thing, I presented myself at 12.30 p.m. sharp and sat down upon a tiny chair in the crowded assembly hall that doubles as a dining-room each lunchtime. The head's word 'mysteries' was just about right. The only ingredient that I recognized was diced carrots, although there was also a brown, leathery creation that could have been anything from Bovril-stained Hovis to fossilized mince.

All went fairy well until 'afters' was served. I had jam roly-poly – without jam. It was while I was exploring this delicacy that Tracey, a particularly unwholesome six-year-old whose left knicker-leg hung a good two inches below her skirt, decided to give me a sticky kiss. Suddenly it was like the Beatles at London Airport. Within seconds every other five- to seven-year-old – boys as well as girls – decided to emulate the baggy-drawered Tracey. I instantly realized why I had no jam in my roly-poly: the kids had had it all. They were absolutely covered with the stuff. At least they were until they kissed me, then a fair proportion of it was transferred to my face, tunic and shirt collar.

I was finally reprieved from this sticky adulation by a young teacher. 'Would you like tea or coffee?' she asked. 'There's very little difference, actually. Or if you wish, you can have a farewell sherry in the staffroom, plus a good wash in the cloakroom,' she added, studying my neck.

With three other schools to visit, I decided not to risk any more passionate academic lunches. I therefore confined these remaining goodbyes to the daily assembly. Even here there were to be problems. Ron Preston, head of a local primary school and by now a good friend, decided on a more theatrical farewell. The whole school – staff and pupils – was assembled in the hall and I was to appear from behind a curtain to, we hoped, thunderous applause. As we stood just out of sight of the children, waiting for the last class to file into the hall, Ron had what he considered an excellent idea.

'What hymn would you like? The children will sing it for you as a going-away treat.'

'Hymn?'

'Yes – hymn. What's your favourite hymn?'

This was like listening to a comedian telling jokes for an entire evening and trying to remember *one* the next day.

'I – er, I don't know any,' I bleated.

'You don't know any?' he echoed incredulously. 'But everyone knows a hymn, surely?'

'Well, yes, I know *some*, I suppose, it's just that I can't think of any right at this moment.'

Peeping through the curtains, we watched as the last of the children settled into place.

'C'mon, it's your last chance,' urged Ron.

Suddenly a title from my own primary school days flashed into mind.

'"Fight the Good Fight",' I requested, with obvious relief.

'Fight the – they won't know that!'

'Oh – well, can't I choose a carol?'

He grimaced. 'Well, if you *have* to I suppose. Which one do you like best?'

'I think it's called "If I Was a Poor Man".'

He shook his head in genuine despair. 'Its proper name is "In the Deep Midwinter". You can't possibly have that – it's only five days till Easter!'

'Well, you did say I could choose a carol,' I pointed out. 'Anyway, I've just remembered a hymn. How about "All People that on Earth Do Dwell"?'

'That's donkey's years old! Good heavens, man, don't you know any new ones?'

As I concentrated hard we could hear the children becoming restless from the other side of the curtain.

'Isn't there one about a "Dance" or something? I quite like that.'

'Yes, of course! "Lord of the Dance". Quite appropriate for Easter, actually. The children will enjoy singing that.'

We slipped through the curtains and to my immense pleasure received a great cheer. Ron raised his hands for silence and slipped into his short speech. '. . . . and so, in addition to this parting gift to him, I have suggested that the school would like to sing PC Cole's very favourite hymn. He immediately chose "Lord of the Dance".'

I watched him carefully as he made this announcement. He never even had his fingers crossed – and him a headmaster too!

After such a long time on the manor, the news of my leaving caused many local people to stop me in the street and wish me well in my retirement. Or even more usual, to reminisce about long dead years. I found many of these conversations fascinating. Local villains who had never had reason to like police and, in fact, never had, suddenly became quite nostalgic for the 'old days'. 'We might 'ave been on opposite sides of the fence, Ginger-boy, but we always respected each other, didn't we?' The fact that they still called me 'Ginger' unarguably dated them. I had not had sufficient hair to be called by that name for fifteen years! There seemed little point in destroying their illusions, so I usually agreed, 'Yes, we did have the greatest respect for each other,' and 'Yes, we did share a great camaraderie.'

The most difficult of these observations to swallow was that put forward by 'Big Bill' Perkins. 'You all had your jobs to do, Ginger, and I for one respected you fellows for it. When I read what goes on nowadays with all this violence and muggings and such like – well, I wonder what we're all coming to, really I do.'

The first time I met Bill was twenty years before, when he had picked up a colleague of mine and tried to kill him, first by strangulation and then by hurling him from the fourth-floor balcony of a block of flats! Time, it seemed, had healed all of Bill's wounds, even the seven years he collected for attempted murder!

'You're right, Bill,' I agreed, with marked lack of courage. 'They *were* good days.'

I suppose all occupations have their myths. The one which recurred most often in these farewells was the myth of the old coppering street-fighter. In one conversation after another I would be asked what had happened to 'Old Wassisname, you remember – big bloke, 'e was'. This stalwart apparently never arrested anyone in his entire service. Instead he would challenge outlawing desperados to a fist fight. 'Jackets off!' he would order. 'Just you and me round the back.' Both participants would retire to a local alley and there the forces of good would triumph over the forces of evil. Each person who recited the story would claim to have known this dragon-slayer personally yet could never quite remember his name. 'You *must've* known 'im, Ginger. Big bloke, 'e was,' was about as close to a name as I could get.

In many respects the saddest farewell for me was Maggie Quinn's. I still called her Maggie Quinn although she had been Maggie Pinnock for twenty-six years. I first met Mag when I was called to a fight at her wedding-party. Miss Quinn had been one of nature's beautiful people. Everything about her shone. She looked so clean and healthy she should have made milk commercials. Her glorious red hair hung down to the small of her back and her wide, white-toothed smile topped an absolutely stunning figure. Yet more than anything else, I admired her vibrant personality. Maggie could have been a cover-girl on glossy magazines and cruise brochures. Instead she married Ryan Pinnock. Everyone knew that Ryan was a drunken brute of a man who would ultimately drag her down to his level. Everyone knew – except Maggie, of course.

Now, twenty-six years after I had first been struck with her astonishing beauty, we had our final conversation. Life had not been good to Maggie. Of her three children, twenty-five-year-old Desmond was serving five years for blackmail, twenty-three-year-old Karen lived in a lesbian squat at King's Cross, and Angela was a twenty-year-old whore going on forty-five. Maggie retained little of her glorious hair, and had not a tooth in her head. She smelt like a polecat and the fat hung from her in great bulbous layers. She had, quite simply, given up.

I had been so preoccupied with my departure from the police that at first I failed to notice the deterioration in my mother's health. By then she lived next door to me, but she had recently commented that she had seen more of me when she lived some eight miles distant. On the last day of my police service, she attended the local hospital for a routine check on her lungs. They decided to keep her in and I called in to visit her on my way to my party. She seemed quite cheerful and wished me luck.

The party itself was an enormous success, with some two hundred friends taking part. It drew to a reluctant close around 3.30 a.m. I had planned to sleep at a friend's house nearby, so had not taken my car. In fact I could have driven with no problems at all: I had spent so long in conversations that I had barely finished a drink all evening. I was, however, particularly tired, and fell on to his settee at four o'clock. I have never wakened so reluctantly. I could feel my arm being tugged and my shoulders shaken but I wanted no part of it.

'C'mon, wake up! Wake up!'

I came up through layer after layer of warm woolly sleep but there still seemed dozens more. The supreme mental effort of muttering the words 'I'm tired' exhausted me and I slipped back into welcoming oblivion. Again I was shaken, once more I struggled into consciousness. This time I managed partially to open my eyes and saw that my tormentor was in a uniform of some description.

'Go away,' I groaned. 'I want to sleep. I'm a civilian.'

But he would not go away. The pulling and shaking increased. I opened my eyes and found myself looking up into the anxious face of Chris McNeil, a colleague from the station.

'Are you awake?' asked Chris. 'Can you hear me?'

'What's the bloody time?'

'It's half past four – listen!' He raised his hand to stop the protest that had already formed on my lips. 'You must go immediately to Hither Green Hospital. Your mother is dying.'

For a moment I could not understand what my mother was doing in hospital when she should have been at home in bed. Slowly, oh so slowly, pieces drifted into place.

'Come on,' said Chris, 'I'll run you there.'

Less than five hours after becoming a civilian I climbed again into the front seat of a police car. Chris tried hard to make conversation but I just stared vacantly through the windscreen at the damp April night. I was no longer tired but I could not assemble my thoughts into a cohesive pattern. After a while I gave up trying. We picked up Joan en route and in less than an hour we stood at my mother's hospital bedside. There was just a small shielded lamp shining down on her bed. Snores and phlegm-rattled throats echoed in the embracing darkness of that bronchial ward.

I looked down at the bed in sheer disbelief. Surely this was not my mother? Yesterday she had been a smart, well-dressed lady, immaculately attired without a hair out of place. Her cheeks had been rosy and her eyes bright. Now, a hundred years older, surrounded by pumps, tubes, wires and bells, here was a gasping, masked creature that bore little resemblance to anyone I knew.

Her eyes flickered open for a second and her lips, barely visible through the plastic mask, moved slowly. 'Hope . . . I . . . didn't . . . spoil . . . your . . . party . . .'

'No, Mum, don't worry,' I assured her. 'It's finished. The party's over.'

Harry Cole

POLICEMAN'S PROGRESS

Being one of four policemen coping with the drunken, sex-mad, middle-aged, pear-shaped Clara, or sitting out a night with the neighbourhood ghost, or calming wayward Rosie, the local prostitute, who'd had her 'Bristols' bitten, must have been a lot more fun than digging out the late and seventy-year-old Elsie Morton, rotting in bed after not being seen for some weeks, dealing with violence, or bearing the news of fatal accidents to bereaved families.

PC Harry Cole, now nearly thirty years on the Southwark force, has done it all and there's consequently many a tale to tell. He produces his account of life on the beat with a combination of good humour and honesty that makes *Policeman's Progress* a rich mixture of riotous and serious reading. Harry Cole's loyalty to the force, but also his obvious sympathy for all reasonable human eccentricities, make one feel that he would be a good man to have around when there's trouble.

Harry Cole

POLICEMAN'S LOT

It's a policeman's lot to be involved with eccentric human behaviour and bizarre happenings, with personal dramas and social occasions, accidental disasters and deliberate wrong-doings. PC Cole, after nearly thirty years on the beat, has seen it all; and whether he's investigating the case of the exploding sewer cover or refereeing at a drunken Irish party, withstanding the abuse of the Gay Liberation Front or sorting out the imaginary fears of a lonely old man, it's his sense of humour that often seems the saving grace.

Fontana Paperbacks: Non-fiction

Fontana is a leading paperback publisher of non-fiction, both popular and academic. Below are some recent titles.

- [ ] CAPITALISM SINCE WORLD WAR II Philip Armstrong, Andrew Glyn and John Harrison £4.95
- [ ] ARISTOCRATS Robert Lacey £3.95
- [ ] PECULIAR PEOPLE Patrick Donovan £1.75
- [ ] A JOURNEY IN LADAKH Andrew Harvey £2.50
- [ ] ON THE PERIMETER Caroline Blackwood £1.95
- [ ] YOUNG CHILDREN LEARNING Barbara Tizard and Martin Hughes £2.95
- [ ] THE TRANQUILLIZER TRAP Joy Melville £1.95
- [ ] LIVING IN OVERDRIVE Clive Wood £2.50
- [ ] MIND AND MEDIA Patricia Marks Greenfield £2.50
- [ ] BETTER PROGRAMMING FOR YOUR COMMODORE 64 Henry Mullish and Dov Kruger £3.95
- [ ] NEW ADVENTURE SYSTEMS FOR THE SPECTRUM S. Robert Speel £3.95
- [ ] POLICEMAN'S PRELUDE Harry Cole £1.50
- [ ] SAS: THE JUNGLE FRONTIER Peter Dickens £2.50
- [ ] HOW TO WATCH CRICKET John Arlott £1.95
- [ ] SBS: THE INVISIBLE RAIDERS James Ladd £1.95
- [ ] THE NEW SOCIOLOGY OF MODERN BRITAIN Eric Butterworth and David Weir (eds.) £2.50
- [ ] BENNY John Burrowes £1.95
- [ ] ADORNO Martin Jay £2.50
- [ ] STRATEGY AND DIPLOMACY Paul Kennedy £3.95
- [ ] BEDSIDE SNOOKER Ray Reardon £2.95

You can buy Fontana paperbacks at your local bookshop or newsagent. Or you can order them from Fontana Paperbacks, Cash Sales Department, Box 29, Douglas, Isle of Man. Please send a cheque, postal or money order (not currency) worth the purchase price plus 15p per book for postage (maximum postage required is £3).

NAME (Block letters) _____

ADDRESS _____

_____